FO HIS HONOR

Terry Johnson
with
Kay D. Rizzo

Pacific Press Publishing Association
Boise, Idaho
Oshawa, Ontario, Canada

Edited by Jerry D. Thomas
Designed by Tim Larson
Cover design by Tim Larson
Cover photo supplied by Terry Johnson
Typeset in 10/12 Century Schoolbook

Library of Congress Cataloging-in-Publication Data

Johnson, Terry, 1966-
For his honor: from schoolroom failure to White House
Honor Guard, Terry Johnson's witness for Christ / Terry
Johnson with Kay D. Rizzo.
     p.   cm.
IBSN 0-8163-1070-X
1. Johnson, Terry,1966- . 2. Seventh-day Adventists—
United States—Biography. I. Rizzo, Kay D. 1943- . II. Title.
BX6193.J63A3   1992
286.7'092—dc20   91-853
[B]   CIP

92 93 94 95 96 • 5 4 3 2 1

Contents

Dedication

This book is dedicated in loving memory to
my sister,
Linda Fay Johnson,
and
in living memory to
my mother and my grandmother,
Zelma Johnson Norman
and
Grezell Settlers

I owe special thanks to . . .

William Norman . . . You believed in me.
Brenda, Louis, Shirley, and Kenner, Jr. . . . You were always there for me.
Glennie Butler and the Sharon church family . . . Your prayers got through loud and clear.
Elder Floyd Matula . . . You are my mentor, my friend.
Elder Don and Ruthie Jacobson and the ministerial staff of the Oregon Conference . . . For your confidence in me.
Pastor Wintley and Linda Phipps and the Capitol Hill Church . . . You encouraged me when I needed it most.
Elder and Mrs. Scales, Sr., and Elder and Mrs. Scales, Jr. . . . Your guidance and advice made the difference.
USAF Senior Master Sergeant Ralph Griffey . . . For your friendship.
USAF Honor Guard Commander John C. Ufford . . . This wouldn't have happened without your faith in me.
Dr. DeWitt Williams, Clarence Hodges, T. Marshall Kelly.

In my heavenly Father's service,

Terry Lyndon Johnson

Foreword

The great need of the world in this closing decade of the twentieth century is the need for role models for youth; adults who are living youthful, inspiring lives. Victims of socio-economic difficulties imposed by external circumstances need to see a real overcomer and a model who not only respects the rules of life, but who uses those societal rules to succeed. Terry Johnson is one such role model.

Many adults are overwhelmed by the stresses and challenges they encounter daily. They need to see inspiring enthusiasm that never gives up, never stops smiling, and never takes its focus off the prize of tomorrow's promise. Terry Johnson is that youthful, living inspiration who knows how to combine diligence and faith to turn dreams into reality.

Whether at the White House as a military honor guard displaying skill and discipline before world leaders or counseling friends and fellow members of the guard, Terry shows his love for all people and for God.

This book will show you how to exercise courage when faced with challenges, faith when faced with overwhelming odds, love when faced with hatred, and humility when faced with success. It is an honor to be a friend of Terry Johnson.

Clarence E. Hodges
Former U.S. Commissioner for
Children and Families and
Deputy Assistant Secretary,
U.S. Department of State

Introduction

Remember the Horatio Alger stories? My even suggesting them could reveal my age. But their heart-touching descriptions of someone poor—born of adversity—making good, always brought a glow to your heart.

Terry's story has some of these characteristics . . . but so, so much more. His triumph over odds such as class disctinction and crippling dyslexia will lift you up and inspire you.

And no TV sitcom writer could think of more humorous plots than arise out of Terry's simple but thrilling ascent from a hopeful mother's dream through to the White House in Washington.

Well, not the presidency. Not yet, anyway! But Terry's splendid achievements will be a shining example for other young people, especially disadvantaged young people, across the country.

Terry's faith and his untamable desire to witness to God's goodness make his story a lasting inspiration. The fascinating account of his full and fruitful young life will be a cherished memory by all who read these pages.

Don't be ashamed of an occasional tear . . . and a sparkle in your eye . . . and a smile on your lips. They are all a part of watching this young man follow in the footsteps of Jesus.

George E. Vandeman
Director, *It Is Written*

Lackland Air Force Base
San Antonio, Texas
Summer 1985

Chapter One

Airman Terry Johnson peered through the plexiglass window as the commercial jet circled San Antonio's International Airport. He eyed the sprawling urban oasis in the middle of Texas cattle country. The green of carefully cultivated lawns and palm tree–lined avenues punctuated the otherwise summer-browned terrain. The late-afternoon sun illuminated a scattering of small rocky hills, instead of the elegant whipped cream–topped peak of Mt. Hood back home in Portland. He glanced across the aisle at the four young men traveling with him and wondered if they felt as homesick and apprehensive as he.

The plane landed and taxied to the terminal. Once the airport personnel maneuvered the metal staircase up to the silver-and-red aircraft, herd instinct prevailed. The passengers spewed forth onto the sizzling pavement and into the air terminal, where they collected their luggage. Assigned point person for the group, Terry consulted his instruction list, then led the way to the prescribed waiting area. Once there, he breathed deeply and smiled to himself. He had a good feeling about this entire adventure. He knew God planned to use him in a special way during his term in the military. Already, he thought, patting the military packets in his coat pocket, I've been assigned responsibility.

He glanced at his watch—9:30 p.m., exactly nine-and-one-half hours since they'd left Portland International Airport. He wondered how long they'd have to wait before the buses arrived from Lackland Air Force Base. He placed his suitcase and travel bag on the floor beside an empty seat overlooking the airfield, sat down, yawned, and stretched.

During the next three hours, more recruits arrived from different parts of the United States. At 12:30 a.m. four green, flat-nosed military buses pulled up in front of the waiting area. A uniformed sergeant hopped out of the last bus. He ordered the men to line up and number off by fours.

A female bus driver stepped up behind the sergeant and bellowed, "All 'ones,' get your bags and get on board the first bus. Move it, move it!" As he climbed on board, Terry cast a sideways glance at the woman. She might not be military, he thought, but she's sure tough enough to be. The faces of the other recruits reflected the same apprehension Terry felt as he found a seat midway back in the bus and sat down.

A half-hour later, the buses arrived at the base and were waved through the checkpoint. Terry's bus pulled to a stop in front of a long row of barracks, shrouded in darkness. The other buses stopped a distance behind them, lost among alien shadows. The recruits climbed out of the bus into the face of a bantam rooster in uniform. The sergeant expanded his chest importantly. "Find your luggage and set it over by the wall."

Terry and the other men pawed through the stack of luggage for their own belongings and placed them next to the adobe brick wall as ordered. As the military bus disappeared into the night, the sergeant shouted for them to line up. The frightened men scrambled into a semblance of a line. Strutting back and forth in front of them, the sergeant sneered at the men's attempt to come to attention, then, as if deciding they weren't worth the bother, marched them to the mess hall. Once inside the building, the exhausted recruits gratefully gulped down hot coffee, buttered toast, cold cereal, and milk while the sergeant spun tales about how tough the training instructors can make life for the cadets.

Fifteen minutes later, he ordered the men outside onto a patio. The fifty men fell into line ten across, five rows deep, as ordered. Terry remembered the advice family members and friends had given him before he left Oregon. "Don't volunteer for anything and remain as inconspicuous as possible," they'd warned.

For the gregarious eighteen-year-old, that sounded simple enough. No problem. I can do that, he thought, consciously situating himself sixth man from the end, three rows back. Light shining out of the small window in the upper third of a door glared into the men's eyes as they stood at attention, awaiting further orders.

Terry nervously clenched and unclenched his fists and stared straight ahead. Despite the exceptionally long day, the adrenalin surged through him as he waited. His first day in the United States Air Force! He'd imagined what it would be like ever since he and his buddies from the Christian high school stopped just for laughs at the air force recruiting booth in Mall 205. The air force recruiter had listened to and asked all the appropriate questions of each of them. When he discovered Terry wanted to become a minister, he suggested Terry join the force and attend assistant chaplain school.

"We usually don't take kids straight out of high school. The air force prefers for them to have a couple of years of college first." The recruiter explained about the tests the boys would have to take before being eligible to join the air force. "We only want the cream of the crop."

Terry cringed. Cream of the crop? He'd never done well in school. Oh, well, he thought, so much for that idea. Why he took the test anyway, he didn't know. And in spite of his poor scholastic record, he passed. After completing the paperwork, he was told he'd have a six-month wait before his induction.

Teachers and friends tried to dissuade Terry and his friends from going through with their plans to enlist. Terry talked with his mother, and together they prayed about his decision. When it came down to actually signing up, his friends backed out. And, instead of six months, the air force called Terry two weeks after his high-school graduation.

The night before leaving home, he prayed again about his decision. A special confidence filled him as if God were telling him to go ahead. The words of Hebrews 13:5 rang in his head. "Never will I leave you; never will I forsake you" (NIV). The next morning, as Terry waited with his mother and stepfather for his flight to be announced, his mother admitted she had experienced the same sense of assurance over his decision.

"I can't explain it. Even as I knelt beside my bed, arguing with God, He filled me with a strange peace." She smiled and patted his face tenderly. "God will go with you, son."

Standing in the darkness waiting for his new life to begin, Terry pushed the thoughts of mother and home to the back of his mind.

Mating crickets dared to break the silence of the sleeping military base. The hot and restless Texas winds swirled about just beyond his immediate attention. Terry wasn't sure when he first noticed the strange tic-tic-tic-tic sound approaching from the stairs beyond the door. But as the clicks grew louder, all other noises faded into the shadows. The men strained to catch a glimpse of the creature making the sound. They could make out something or someone coming down the steps—feet, legs, body. When a man's neck filled the entire view through the window, Terry's eyes widened with uncertainty, and he thought, This guy must be huge, whoever he is.

The door swung open. The gigantic silhouette of a man wearing a "Smokey the Bear" hat filled the doorway. As he stepped into the light, the man spelled regulation military from his rigid blond crew cut to his piercing, arctic blue eyes to his grim, no-nonsense mouth and granite-chiseled, square jaw. Six-feet-six and well over 250 pounds, the man paused to allow the full impact of his enormity to sink in; then he swaggered forward to the center of the concrete patio. His stance exuded arrogance and disdain as he stood with legs spread and hands on his hips.

"I am your training instructor, Staff Sergeant Collier. For the next six weeks, I am your mother and your father. You will do everything I say. Is that clear?"

Without instruction, the men answered in unison, "Yes, sir!"

"I can't hear you," the T.I. taunted, looking straight at Terry.

Again the men shouted, "Yes, sir!"

He strode toward Terry, his eyes never wavering from his target, his upper lip curling into a sneer. Pushing people aside like discarded cornstalks, he plowed through the lineup until he stood nose to nose with the stunned cadet.

"I didn't realize the military was so hard up for people. Look at you! You're the poorest excuse for a cadet that I've ever seen." Terry's eyes grew wider with each word the sergeant screamed into his face.

Terry swallowed hard; sweat beaded on his brow as the man continued to yell. "I can't believe this—the military must be desperate. Where's your bags, slick? Grab your bags. Point your bags out to me!"

Terry's throat closed; the words stung. His hand shook as he pointed to his luggage standing against the wall.

"Where's the bus that brought you? I want you to go back home!" He forced the young cadet to pick up his luggage. "Now run, flyboy! Catch that bus!"

Terry stumbled down the empty street in the direction the sergeant pointed, trying to catch a nonexistent bus at one o'clock in the morning. He knew it would be impossible to catch up with the bus. Halfway down the block, he called back over his shoulder, "The bus left thirty minutes ago."

Running behind him like a trained attack dog, Staff Sergeant Collier ignored the cadet's protest and shouted, "Run faster. Catch it."

It had been a long, exhausting day. Terry stumbled over his own feet to obey the command, but in spite of his efforts, he started slowing down. Yet the sergeant continued barking at his heels. "Catch that bus, airman!" Startled at the man's close proximity, Terry bounded forward with his last burst of energy.

"Lord," Terry prayed as he ran, "this can't be right. I just got here, Lord! I dedicated myself to You, and You're letting problems like this happen?" Before he realized it, only the sound of his own footsteps echoed in the night. The T.I. had returned to the rest of the flight unit left standing at attention on the patio.

When Terry was certain he couldn't run another step, he

heard the sergeant yell, "Come on back. Come on back here." Gasping for every breath, the cadet turned around. The training instructor continued his tirade. "You ought to be glad that bus is gone 'cause you would sure be on it!" Terry stumbled back to the group and dropped his bags on the concrete beside him. In spite of his tired, aching muscles and the sweat pouring from his body, he drew himself to attention.

The sergeant strode over until he was nose to nose once more. "Too bad that bus left. That's the only reason I'm letting you stay here. I'll let you stay the night, but tomorrow, you're gonna be on the bus out of here. You hear me?"

Terry stared straight ahead at the sergeant's wafer-thin, hard lips, his rage held in check by sheer determination. "Yes, sir."

The T.I. glared straight back into his eyes. "I want everybody to get his bags and go upstairs." As the other cadets reached for their luggage, Sergeant Collier pointed at Terry's nose. "Johnson, I want you to stay here."

At the mention of his last name, another piece of advice Terry had received before leaving home popped into his mind. "Never let the sergeant know your name. If the sergeant knows your name, he'll be after you the whole time, especially if he doesn't like you." Five minutes, Terry thought, and already I've blown it on every count.

"Everybody upstairs," the T.I. barked again. "Leave your bags where they are, Johnson. I want you to wait five minutes before you follow us."

The cadets filed through the doorway and up the stairs. At the top of the stairs, they rounded a corner and disappeared from sight. Terry had no idea where they might be headed. He waited the five minutes and slowly, timidly climbed the stairs. The hallway at the top of the stairs was deserted. He looked first one way, then the other. He stared at the dozens of closed doors on each side of the hall.

Where should I go? Terry strode to one door and opened it—a janitor's closet. Well, that can't be it, he thought. He tried to turn the knob on the door across the hall—locked. He walked farther down the hall. "Lord, help me find my unit."

The next door he opened led to a second hallway. He walked down the narrow tiled corridor, his feet pounding the cold floor like punishing fists. Within a few minutes, he opened another door and came face to face with Sergeant Collier and the rest of his flight unit.

The T.I. looked surprised. He waved Terry toward the row of bunks and snarled, "Go to bed, and tomorrow we're gonna start the day off right."

Terry staggered to the opposite side of the room to an unoccupied bunk and fell in. Glancing at his watch, he groaned. Two o'clock in the morning? "Lord, what did You get me into? I'm trying to be faithful, and already You're letting the devil get at me. I just want to quit!"

Splinters of doubt crept under his skin. Many times during his childhood, when pressures threatened to destroy him, Terry Johnson had wanted to quit, to give up, but never more than he did that night as he lay on the lumpy military-issue mattress in the darkness, waiting for and dreading the dawn.

Chapter Two

The child snuggled down under the blankets and willed the world to go away. The voice of his mother standing at the foot of the stairs persisted in breaking through his slumber.

"Terry? Terry! Aren't you out of bed yet? You'd better hustle, child, or you're gonna be late for school again." The seven-year-old boy rolled over in bed and groaned. Outside his northeast Portland bedroom window, a cold drizzle dripped from the eaves of the spacious two-story green-and-white Victorian-style house, creating a watercolor gray world. Due to the heavy rains, the yard behind the six-bedroom house had become one giant swimming hole.

"Terry?" His mother's Creole accent thickened with insistence. "Have you gotten yourself out of that bed yet? Or do I have to come up there and get you up myself?"

"Ma, I don't want to go to school today." He threw back the covers and stepped out onto the cold hardwood floor. "I don't feel so good." Whenever he thought of going back to Mrs. Pennyworth's classroom, his stomach churned with anger.

"You've used that excuse one too many times, young man!" He heard her tread on the stairs seconds before she burst into his room. Her eyes flashed as she shook a cooking spatula at him. "Terry Lyndon Johnson, you get yourself dressed! You are going to school if I have to take you there myself."

Defeated, the boy hauled on his jeans and plain sport shirt, then dragged himself down to the kitchen. He stared into his cereal bowl, slapping the milk against the golden flakes with his spoon until they turned to a soggy mush.

"Mama, I don't want to go back to that school ever again. Please don't make me." They'd had this conversation before. "My teacher don't like me."

"*Doesn't* like you, not *don't* like you." She slipped into her heavy plaid wool coat, then handed him his insulated sky jacket. "You gotta go to school, Terry. You gotta get an education in order to make something of yourself."

"I-I-I don't like school . . ." Terry muttered as they stepped out into the typical Oregon winter rains.

Impatient, she urged him to the family car. "Maybe today will be different," she encouraged. Terry shook his head and fell into step beside her. Having to deliver Terry right to the door of the school made it difficult to get to work on time.

When they arrived at the school, his mother parked the car and got out. She came around to the passenger side of the car and opened the door. The child slid down lower in the seat. "I don't want to go!"

"Well, you have to." Tugging at his coat sleeve, she urged him from the car and up the front steps of the building. Once inside, she straightened his jacket and planted a kiss on his forehead. "Now, son, you be a good boy today, OK? For me?"

His chin drooped onto his jacket zipper as he looked up into her eyes for one pleading minute longer. She scowled. When he knew there'd be no reprieve, he shuffled toward his classroom door, where the other second-graders were lining up.

It happened before the first bell rang. An argument broke out. No one knew who started it or why. First one boy shoved the boy in front of him; then that boy shoved back. Within seconds, all of the boys in the line were pushing and shoving one another while the girls squealed with displeasure. That's when Mrs. Pennyworth's pinched-up little face appeared around the doorjamb.

"Quiet! I will have it quiet!" the teacher shouted, her eyes flashing with fury directly at Terry. She grabbed the startled boy by the shoulder and shook him, screaming into his face. "You are nothing but a troublemaker, Terry Johnson!"

The child stared, fascinated, at the woman's tight little gray curls bobbing about on her head and shaking to the same rhythm she'd applied to his shoulder. At the same time she pointed her long, bony finger at his nose.

"Are you paying attention to me?" Nodding in fear, he stared up into her watery eyes, certain his life must be over.

He was in trouble again with Mrs. Pennyworth. He was always in trouble with Mrs. Pennyworth. Big for his size and one of the first group of black children to be integrated into the primarily white elementary-school district of Irvington, Terry took the brunt of the blame for any scuffle, fight, or disturbance that occurred in the classroom or out. If he was involved, he started it. If he watched, he should have stopped it since he was bigger than the rest of the children. Whenever the boy tried to speak out to defend himself, fright would convert his words into a jumble of unintelligible noises. When the other students defended him, she ignored their claims, insisting he was nothing but a no-good troublemaker.

With this daily pattern of abuse, Terry began to believe his teacher. He was stupid. He was a troublemaker. He was bad, so why even try to be good?

When the other children practiced the alphabet, Mrs. Pennyworth gave Terry a coloring book and announced to the class, "Terry is allowed to color because he's retarded. He can't learn his letters."

Choosing up sides for spelling bees became a nightmare. In a class of forty or more children, he would always be chosen last. Amid tittering and laughter from the other students and from the teacher, the two captains would argue about who was going to get stuck with "dumb old Terry" this time. Anger would boil up inside Terry, and one time he punched one of the captains and got sent home. The teacher would later record the incident in his official school record. "Terry is a very angry child, very disturbed, and had to be sent home."

But a worse nightmare than spelling bees was reading class, when she forced him to stand up front and read out loud. The woman knew he couldn't read. Reading silently was difficult—those squiggly black letters on the page made no sense to him whatsoever—but to read aloud in front of his classmates was totally beyond the child's ability. Sometimes when he was singled out to read aloud, he would pretend to be sick or to have to go to the bathroom.

One day, Mrs. Pennyworth ordered him to read in front of the class. His protests and evasions fell on deaf ears. Pursing her lips into a prim little smile, she looked down her razor-thin nose at the boy. "Terry, go up to the front of the room and read aloud, starting on page 132."

The child recoiled and pressed his body against the back of his seat. His dark brown eyes widened in desperation. Read? In front of everyone? His face reddened. His heart pounded with terror. The woman became insistent.

"I can't," he whispered, his words unintelligible. "Please don't make me, Mrs. Pennyworth."

A look of smug satisfaction crossed the woman's face as her eyes narrowed to furious slits. "What's wrong? Are you stupid or something, that you can't read? I told you to read. Now!"

Blotches of angry color scaled his neck as he arose to his feet, picked up his reading book, and walked to the front of the room. When he turned to face his classmates, one of the girls had begun to giggle. Mrs. Pennyworth struggled to swallow her own grin.

"No!" His lower lip protruded, then clamped firmly shut in a sullen frown.

The woman's face hardened; anger glinted in her flashing eyes. She marched up the aisle toward him. "I said—" Shooting a terrified glance at his teacher, the boy grabbed one of the wooden kiddie chairs beside the teacher's desk and threw it. It skidded across the floor toward his teacher.

"Leave me alone," he gasped, the words so tiny and forced, even he might have imagined them. Terry bounded from the room, the door slam echoing down the terrazzo-tiled hallway. "I won't go to school, I won't!" He headed down two flights of stairs until he reached the basement. He tiptoed past the furnace room, where the janitor sat leaning back in his reclining desk chair reading the morning paper. Carefully he hurried down the long hallway and ducked into a broom closet. Scrunching himself into a tiny ball in the corner, he awaited the sound of the closing bell.

After supper that evening, Terry learned that his mother had heard about his behavior in school. As she sat down to talk, Terry tried to explain what was happening in Mrs. Pennyworth's classroom.

His mother shook her head slowly. "Terry, why do you say such things? Your teacher wouldn't do that to you."

The boy looked up into his mother's eyes. His warm eyes filled with pleading. "She did. It's true, Mama. It's true."

The child's tales seemed so fantastic, so exaggerated. No teacher would act that way. "Son, what am I to do with you?"

Daily encounters with his teacher and his resulting truancy continued. He didn't mind his trips to the principal's office. He liked the kindly faced woman with the laughing brown eyes. She talked with him, asked him questions, and actually listened to his answers.

Whenever a film was being shown in the classroom, Mrs. Pennyworth made Terry sit in the hall until it was over. Whenever the class went on a field trip, the teacher barred him from going unless his mother accompanied him. And since his mother had to work all day, he seldom got to go. It was a rare day when Mrs. Pennyworth didn't give him a note to take home to his mother. The child didn't want always to be in trouble, but he didn't know how to stop it.

One day, after he'd managed to survive the entire six hours without hassle, his teacher handed him an envelope, instructing him to give it to his mother. Terry cast a baleful glare at the long white envelope. He tried to recall what bad things he might have done that day. But he could think of nothing. Yet he'd learned long ago that letters from the school meant trouble. He considered dropping the letter in a storm drain on the way home but changed his mind, since the last time he'd done that, his mother had grounded him.

He trudged the seven blocks home, waved to the next-door neighbor lady so she would know he'd reached home safely, then let himself inside the big, empty house. He placed the letter on the kitchen table. Oh, well, he reasoned, what more can Mrs. Pennyworth do to me that she hasn't already done?

Chapter Three

Terry sat on the front steps of his house, slumped over into a glob of misery. His mother had come home from work and read the letter. She hadn't stopped wringing her hands and crying since. He hated Mrs. Pennyworth for making his mother cry. When his twenty-two-year-old sister, Linda, arrived home, he overheard his mother telling her about the letter. She used words like *banned from Oregon's schools, mentally incompetent, psychologists, McClaren's School for the Mentally Disabled, severely disturbed, reevaluated at eighteen, reenter society.* Terry didn't know what they meant, but he knew they must be pretty awful to upset everyone so.

"I don't care what the teacher or the superintendent of schools says," Terry's sister insisted. "My little brother is not retarded. I know."

That word Terry did understand—*retarded*—as well as the words *dummy* and *troublemaker.* Mrs. Pennyworth had made certain of that. He smiled to himself. He liked having his sister, Linda, stick up for him. She'd tell that nasty old teacher a thing or two!

"It's impossible!" Linda, the nearest in age of his five siblings, had finished high school at sixteen and immediately gone on to complete her two-year nurse's training. "When I take him to restaurants, he has perfect manners, uses the right forks and everything. And look at the way he memorizes the newscast every night. What seven-year-old do you know who would prefer watching Walter Cronkite to Bullwinkle cartoons?"

19

It was true. Terry never had problems at home. Cartoons and other kiddie programs bored him. In the evenings, while his mother prepared supper, he would sit on the floor in the kitchen and watch the evening news. At the end of each newscast, Terry would ask his mother questions about what he'd seen and heard but hadn't understood. When it came to government and politics, he had total recall. His mother loved showing off her little political prodigy at Sunday dinners.

Since the Johnson home was bigger than most of the homes of the Portland Maranatha Church members, it became a gathering point after the Sunday-morning services. Deacons, elders, pastors, and friends assembled for one of Zelma's famous southern dinners. Mounds of mashed potatoes with butter melting down the sides, bowls of boiled greens and black-eyed peas, tender slices of turkey smothered in gravy, and homemade biscuits tempted even the most reluctant appetite.

As family and friends flocked around the table, Zelma would say, "Terry, tell us why there's no sugar on the table," or "Terry, tell us about the gas shortage." The seven-year-old would rattle off the answers to the latest news item like a sportscaster reporting the NBA basketball scores.

The Watergate scandal fascinated him. He watched, as if in a trance, while the commentators reported the latest events breaking around the beleaguered president and his advisors. Ehrlichman, Colson, Mitchell—Terry knew all the names of the participants and how each man was involved in the unfolding scandal.

Neither Zelma nor her daughter could accept the teacher's evaluation of Terry. But they didn't understand how someone so bright could have so much trouble learning to read and spell.

"Mom," Linda insisted, "we can't give up on Terry. We can't put him away in some school for the mentally retarded, no matter what anyone says!"

Put him away? Terry shuddered. What terrible thing did a person have to do to be put away?

"He's banned from the public school system." His mother

reread the letter through another storm of tears. "The state will take him away if I don't send him to school somewhere. The experts say he'll never go beyond fourth grade, that he should learn a trade so that he can possibly reenter society as an adult." Terry couldn't figure out what all the fuss was about. He didn't like school anyway.

Linda broke Terry's temporary bubble of happiness. "What about private schools? Can you get Terry into one of those?"

"I don't know, but I'm sure going to try."

Terry's mother refused to give up. She went to see Dr. Bates, a child psychologist and the principal of the Irvington school. The doctor admitted that she'd never had a minute's trouble with Terry. Instead, she found the child delightful to talk with whenever he was sent to her office. Dr. Bates contacted the Columbia Christian School, and they agreed to take him on probation if he would repeat the second grade.

There, Terry met Mrs. Shurlock, a determined teacher who refused to accept defeat in anything. Whenever Terry said, "I can't," she would say, "Yes you can. With God, you can do anything!"

For weeks, Mrs. Shurlock kept Terry after school to help him learn how to make his ABC's. At the same time, she worked with him on his speech impediment. "Take your time, Terry. Think about what you wish to say and then say it." Slowly, as his basic academic skills developed, his self-confidence grew, and his negative behavior disappeared.

One of the requirements of the Columbia Christian School was for all students to read the Bible through every year. Each day the students had specific chapters to study. Terry struggled through page after page of words that made little sense. The next day, when the teacher discussed the assignment, Terry would hear and understand what he had attempted to read. Along with the daily Bible readings, the students memorized complete chapters. Terry persisted, and within a few months, Mrs. Shurlock recommended him for the next grade level. She wrote on his report card, "Terry is so helpful in the classroom. He tries so hard to please."

In the third grade, his teacher spurred Terry's interest in

politics. For the presidential elections, she divided the class into two teams. Each team was to research one of the two major presidential candidates, Ford and Carter. The teams brought in newspaper clippings and magazine articles. With the help of his mother, Terry wrote letters to the Democratic headquarters in Portland, asking for information about Jimmy Carter. Instead of a handful of brochures glorifying the candidate, Terry received a personally signed letter from Jimmy Carter himself. When Mr. Carter won the election, Terry swelled with pride. President Carter's victory had become Terry's victory too.

Terry's being the only black child in the school didn't seem to matter to the teachers or to the other 2,000 students. Terry made friends with a Swedish boy named Bill whose father had recently died. Bill's mother appreciated the refined manners Terry had learned from his sister, Linda, and encouraged her son to associate with him. On weekends she would take the two boys to fine restaurants and to their condominium on the coast. Terry's life seesawed between his weekdays hanging out with his black friends in northeast Portland and his weekends with Bill and Bill's mother's wealthy associates during which he learned the social skills that would ultimately shape the direction of his life.

During his fifth-grade year, Terry's mother's best friend, Glennie, became a Seventh-day Adventist and wanted to share her newfound faith with Zelma. After studying the Bible with Glennie, Terry and his mother joined the Sharon Seventh-day Adventist Church, and Terry transferred to Portland Adventist Elementary School.

His new teacher, Mrs. Brooks, supplied Terry with his next tool for success—do it over until you get it right. She refused to accept second-rate work from him. The boy blossomed with each new accomplishment. The first few days, he was certain no one liked him, and he'd never fit in like he had at his last school. But Terry's enthusiasm soon made him a leader in his class. When the grade school's Week of Prayer arrived, his teacher asked him to find someone to speak on one of the mornings.

"You can ask an adult friend or perhaps your pastor," the teacher explained.

The child thought for a moment, then asked, "Can I do it?"

The teacher laughed at the boy's naiveté. "No, Terry, you can't do it."

Terry dropped his head. "But I'd really like to." After discussing it further, the teacher decided to consult with the principal. To their surprise, the man agreed.

The sixth-grader chose to retell his favorite Bible story, David and Goliath. With the confidence of an ordained minister, Terry addressed his peers. "Now, you see the marks I've drawn on the floor?" He pointed to two chalk marks, one on each side of the assembly room. "That's how tall Goliath was." Then he asked the tallest boy and the shortest girl in the entire school to come up front and lie down next to the line. "He was a pretty big guy, huh?" The students laughed.

Terry kept the students and teachers spellbound for an hour and fifteen minutes. He went home after school that night with a new vision. Mrs. Shurlock had been right. God had a special plan for his life, and he was determined to discover what it might be.

Chapter Four

Terry started awake at the shrill blast of morning reveille followed by the rumble of grumbling and swearing from the other forty-nine cadets in his unit. His dream about his family in Portland had popped like a soap bubble. He rubbed his eyes and peered at his wristwatch—five o'clock? A groan escaped his lips. His brain, numbed by too short a night's sleep, scrambled to identify his surroundings—Texas, boot camp, Staff Sergeant Collier! Terry leaped from his bed, banging his head on the upper bunk. He winced, then dashed to the showers.

When he returned to his bunk, he hauled on his civilian clothes. "Help me, Lord. Whatever I did last night to draw attention to myself, help me not to do it again today." As Terry bent down to tie the shoelace on his Nike sneaker, the staff sergeant strode into the room.

"Attention," the sergeant bawled. The hairs on Terry's neck snapped to attention before he did. "First thing this morning is a shakedown search! That's right, a shakedown search." The man continued barking his orders. "Put all your belongings on your beds. Dump your bags and your suitcases in the middle of your bed. Everything!

The sergeant posed, legs spread, with his hands on his hips. "If any of you guys were dumb enough to bring along your private cache of drugs or weapons, don't try to hide 'em from me."

With the bunks arranged in a large rectangle along the four walls of the room, the sergeant chose to begin the search at the farthest one—Terry's. Even though he knew he hadn't brought along any contraband, Terry groaned. Collier spelled trouble for Terry no matter what he did. Pawing through the first cadet's belongings, the training instructor growled, "We had a religious cadet here last time—a Mormon. And this Mormon tried his best to get out of work whenever he could. He even called the elders of his church in to plead his case." The sergeant straightened and cast a malevolent glare at each of the quaking airmen. "And I won't tolerate that nonsense—do you understand? No religious freaks in my unit!"

Terry gulped. Before he left Portland, he had asked his mother to put a Bible and a few good books he might use for witnessing in his suitcase. He wondered what the sergeant would say when he saw the Bible. He wondered what else she might have stuck in the case. He turned and unzipped his first bag. A Bible fell out onto the bed. Then a second Bible hit the bedcovers. A third. A fourth. Four Bibles! Terry maintained his mask of defensive calm as he unzipped the second suitcase. Copies of *Steps to Christ*, like autumn leaves on a windy day, tumbled onto the bed.

"Oh, boy! This guy's going to kill me!" His mouth dropped open as other books and religious pamphlets cascaded from the case. The twenty to twenty-five books in front of him looked like a million to the stunned cadet. Terry glanced about, hoping no one had noticed. He considered his options. If I move, he'll think I'm trying to hide drugs or weapons. If I don't, and he sees the books, I'm dead meat! Maybe I can toss them under the bunk without being seen. Terry inched sideward and with one smooth motion scooped up a handful of the books and a couple of Bibles, tossed them under the bed, then reached for a second batch.

Like a hawk dropping out of the skies toward his unsuspecting prey, the staff sergeant swooped down on the terrified cadet. "Hey, slick! What are you doing? What are you hiding?" Caught with the condemning evidence in hand, Terry swallowed.

"Oh, no, not again! Another religious nut case," Sergeant Collier shrieked and stormed across the barracks, mumbling as he disappeared into his office. "I can't take this. I can't take this. Another religious freak!" The door slammed behind him.

Terry closed his eyes. His days in the military stretched out before him like an impassable road. Chances are, I'll spend most of them in the brig, he thought. He shook his head to clear it. "This is Your will, Lord, for my life? This is my special purpose?" The other airmen glanced at Terry, then at one another. No one dared move until ordered to do so. A few minutes later, Sergeant Collier's assistant appeared to finish the inspection.

From then on, whenever Sergeant Collier needed a scapegoat, Terry was it. If he needed someone to yell at, he chose Terry. If he needed to make an example of anyone—Terry was chosen. The airman suffered a continual stream of mental abuse in the days that followed.

Each night during the first week, Terry lay in his bunk, stared out into the darkness, and prayed, "I don't understand, Lord. I'm trying to be strong. I'm trying to live for You. How can this be happening?" Doubts bombarded his mind. Maybe God hadn't wanted him to join the military. Worse yet, maybe God wasn't with him at all. "Lord, I'll make a deal with You. For one solid week, even though this is the toughest experience I've ever faced, I'm going to be a 100 percent dedicated Christian. No matter how tough it gets," he vowed. "But if this abuse continues beyond this week, I quit. At least I can say I gave Christianity a try."

The following morning, the cadets had just finished making their beds when the staff sergeant burst into the bay and shouted them to attention. The men scrambled to obey. Collier swaggered over to one of the beds and pointed at the edge of the mattress. "Look at this corner! You call this a hospital corner?" he shouted in the frightened owner's face. With one swipe, Staff Sergeant Collier bent down and yanked the covers off the mattress. "Do it again, airman, until you get it right!"

When he reached Terry's bed, the sergeant picked up the bed and flipped the entire bed frame upside down. A laser beam of fury shot from his eyes as he screamed in the young cadet's face. "Johnson, I'm getting rid of you. You do not deserve to be in the military." Then, as if to emphasize his hatred for the young man, he emptied all of Terry's personal possessions from his locker into the middle of the floor. "I am your T.I. I am your god! Remember that, flyboy!" Sergeant Collier whirled about and stormed into his office.

The moment the staff sergeant disappeared, Terry righted and remade his bed. "Try to find something wrong with those corners," he muttered beneath his breath.

"Why, God, why are You allowing this to happen?" As he reorganized his locker according to the diagram he'd been given, he vowed to do everything right so the sergeant would have no cause for censure. After checking the lid of the tooth-paste tube for residue, Terry placed the tube exactly as the diagram indicated. He repolished his military-issued, straight-edged razor to be certain it was clean of all whiskers and water stains, then placed it in the appropriate spot inside the locker. He checked and rechecked every detail before closing the locker door. There's no way the man can complain about my locker now, he told himself.

When Terry returned to his bunk that night, all of his be-longings were again piled in the middle of his bed. There was nothing he could do but go through the two-hour process once again. The next day, he returned from training classes to dis-cover that the sergeant had scrambled everything in his locker. The underwear Terry had so carefully folded into the regulation six-inch square were wrinkled and would have to be pressed again. Throughout the week, the harder Terry tried to perform his duties properly, the more Sergeant Collier harassed him. And the more the staff sergeant harassed him, the more nervous Terry became, and the more mistakes he made. In his efforts to do everything right, Terry lost the ability to march. He couldn't keep in step. Left face, right face, about face, it didn't matter. His brain heard the orders, but his body went ahead and did its own thing.

Because of Terry's marching problems, the staff sergeant nicknamed him "Gomer," after the hapless Gomer Pyle, a TV character from the old "Andy Griffith Show."

"Gomer, you're messin' up again." The staff sergeant's words echoed back and forth in Terry's brain long after the flight left the marching field. In bed at night, he cried out in silent anguish. "Why are You doing this to me, Lord? Why?"

Starving for a sympathetic ear and a generous helping of home-grown logic, he called his mom. When he heard her voice on the telephone, tears welled up in his eyes. He told her his story.

"I'm praying for you, son," she reminded him. "I know that God and you together can do it."

Knowing Terry claimed to be a Christian, the other recruits in his flight watched and listened. Jeff, a born-again Christian from Florida, who belonged to the Assembly of God Church, tried to encourage him. "Hang in there, Terry. God promised to always be with you. He's not going to let you down now."

A streetwise cadet named Tom, who told Terry that his grandmother once attended a Seventh-day Adventist church in Portland, slugged Terry on the arm. "Come on, don't let the man get to ya. Just be cool. You'll make it."

Terry smiled. "Thanks, guys. I know the Lord led me into the air force, but I don't understand Collier's beef with Christians."

Jeff picked up Terry's Bible from his bed and flipped through the pages. "Obviously, God has a plan for you, and Satan is trying to disrupt it. I'm certain that Daniel and his friends weren't feeling too blessed when they were captured and marched to Babylon in chains. It took a while before they understood that they were part of God's plan."

The three airmen talked about God and His plans for the lives of His children. Curious as to what the attraction might be, a few other cadets inched closer to listen. At the end of their discussion, Terry reached into his locker and pulled out a handful of *Steps to Christ*, by Ellen White, and handed one copy to each of the men. "Here are some of those books my mom packed for me. I think there are enough for each of us. If you'd like, we can meet again to learn more about God together."

As the airmen wandered off to prepare for bed, Terry closed his Bible and laid it on the bed beside him. Rick, a cadet whose arrogance irritated the other members of the flight, sat down at the foot of Terry's bed, blocking his exit. "I see you're reading the Bible. What are you reading about?"

Chapter Five

Terry studied the face of the pale young man with steel blue eyes and perpetual sneer. Is Rick seriously interested? Terry wondered. "I'm reading Isaiah 53, the prophecy about how Jesus was wounded for our sins." He stiffened and waited for the cadet's usual quarrelsome remarks.

Instead, the slightly built young man, who strutted about the barracks looking for a fight, seemed genuinely interested. "It's good you're reading about Christ. I've read quite a bit about Him too. In fact, I have a book about Christ that goes on where the Bible leaves off."

Terry cocked his head to one side and frowned. "Oh? I've always understood that the Bible was complete in itself."

"Oh, no," Rick wagged his finger and shook his head. "You can learn all about it in the *Book of Mormon.* I think you'd find it interesting." Terry listened as the cadet warmed up to his subject, stopping long enough to ask Terry questions he couldn't answer. The cadets closest to Terry's bunk eavesdropped on the discussion while Rick grilled Terry on what he believed, stumping him often. Though Rick was generally disliked among the flight members, Terry still felt the embarrassment of being ignorant about his religion.

After the first encounter, Rick intensified his barrage on Terry's professed religion. And instead of talking one on one like the first time, he staged his attacks in front of the entire flight team.

"Your church has a woman prophet. Don't you know the

Bible doesn't condone a woman prophet? And what about this belief of yours that Jesus is coming again?" When Terry tried to answer, Rick twisted his words until they came out entirely different than Terry meant.

After each attack Terry took refuge in his Bible. "I've got to find the answers, Lord. I know what I believe, but I just don't know how to prove it."

Jeff observed Terry's frustration. "Did you know that Rick is writing home to the church elders, asking for ways to stump you? He's not even a practicing Mormon. He's what they call a jack-Mormon!"

Terry shrugged. It doesn't really matter, he thought to himself, who I'm up against, Rick or the elders of the Mormon Church. I need to know what I really believe for me, if for no one else—I'm up against me.

When alone, Terry prayed for wisdom. He remembered his Bible classes at Portland Adventist Academy, in particular, his Bible teacher, Elder Floyd Matula. It had all been there—the Bible truths to support his beliefs. But instead of taking the message to heart, Terry studied to pass tests and quizzes, not to become acquainted with the Saviour.

He fit in with every crowd at the school—the practicing Christians, the party goers, the kids who worked on cars, the computer enthusiasts. It was a heady experience for the one-time second-grader whom no one wanted on their spelling team. With a flourishing social life at the academy, he always had things to do and places to go. While the change charged his ego, it did nothing for his spiritual commitment. Terry knew all the Christian principles. He could still recite entire chapters from the Word of God. But none of the words traveled the eighteen inches from his brain to his heart. He knew about Christ but didn't know Him. Terry's mother agonized over the changes occurring in her son and did the only thing a mother could do—she prayed.

While cognizant of Terry's problems, Elder Matula didn't give up on him. Terry admired the veteran teacher. The man showed a sincere interest in his students. He dared to trust the students of his class, expecting the best from them and

getting it—especially from Terry. Each week the pastor assigned a memory text to his classes. When it came time to
quiz them on it, Elder Matula would often leave the room
while they wrote out the verse. As a result, very few students
ever cheated on the memory-verse quizzes.

If he trusts me so much that he would leave me unattended
while I write out the verse, Terry thought, I sure don't want to
let him down. When he asked Terry to join the seminar group
he sponsored to the local churches, Terry leaped at the chance.
He loved to speak in public.

Terry didn't worry about spending half of the weekend partying with his friends and the other half preaching the gospel.
He liked to preach, and he liked to party. But in time the dual
lifestyle nibbled away at his conscience and his constitution.
After a night of cruising Eighty-second Street with his buddies
and ending up at the city's popular teen hangout, Terry hardly
felt like preaching the Word of God the next morning. Early
Saturday morning, he would call his teacher to beg off.

"Terry, we really need you this morning," Elder Matula
would say. "Come on, come go with us. It will be good for you."

In spite of Terry's hangover, his respect for his teacher and
his desire not to let him down caused the young man to relent.
In the van on the way to the church, Terry would look at his
friend and wonder, Does he know what I did last night? Does
he have any idea what poor excuses for Christians half of the
students really are? He has to! Then why would he want to
waste his weekends on us?

The minister never scolded Terry or put him down. He
acted like nothing was wrong. Their friendship grew. The minister took Terry home with him until the young boy felt almost
like one of the family. In quiet moments together, Elder
Matula would tell Terry, "I see something special in you,
Terry. God has a purpose for your life."

Now, 2,000 miles away from the security of friends and
family, Terry wondered how he could have been so foolish as
to take so much for granted. Now, battered by both the training instructor and Rick, Terry studied God's Word and prayed
for wisdom every free moment of the day and night.

Slowly, almost imperceptibly, he noticed changes—not in Staff Sergeant Collier or in Rick but in himself. He found it easier to counter Rick's charges. And on the training field, instead of allowing his anger to boil over at Collier's goading, Terry learned to smile and answer the sergeant's reprimands with, "Sir, I'll get it taken care of immediately."

The first time this happened, the bewildered sergeant stared in amazement at the smiling cadet as if to say, "Why can't I break this guy? At the very least he should get mad." Frustrated, the sergeant tried again but received the same response—a smile and assurance the error would be rectified. Whenever the sergeant trashed another cadet's locker, Terry took time to help his peer reorganize his belongings.

In spite of the sergeant's harassments, Terry grew stronger, more confident, and closer to God. On Friday of the first week, the training instructors marched the men down to the base chapel, where each of the cadets met with the chaplain representing his preferred church affiliation. Since the six-week cadet training program closed down each weekend, the men were encouraged to attend the religious service of their choice. Church attendance added points in the competition among the flights to become the honor flight of the training session. And Staff Sergeant Collier ached to win the honors.

Terry's flight, along with the men from a number of other flights, filed into the sanctuary. After the last man sat down, an officer walked to the pulpit and introduced himself. "My name is Captain David Thorgoodson. I will be serving those of you airmen who belong to the Seventh-day Adventist Church. This morning, however, I am the chaplain in charge."

Terry snapped alert. Seventh-day Adventist? He'd almost given up hope that he'd find one Seventh-day Adventist while in basic training.

Captain Thorgoodson spoke on the importance of teamwork. He talked about dealing with moments of loneliness and depression. "We, the chaplain staff of Lackland Air Force Base, are here to help you face those moments. But before we can serve you, we need to get acquainted with you. When I announce your denomination, please move to the area of the chapel indicated. Roman Catholic?"

The rows emptied out as the airmen joined the chaplains representing their religious affiliations, leaving in the pews a handful of men who had no church preference and Terry.

Finally, Captain Thorgoodson asked for all Seventh-day Adventists to come down front by the pulpit. Terry inched out of his chair, nervously looking around. No one else joined him as he walked down to meet the Adventist chaplain. The chaplain shook Terry's hand. "So you're a Seventh-day Adventist, Airman Johnson. Where are you from?"

A grin spread across the cadet's face. He'd been so lonely for another friendly face. "Portland, Oregon, sir."

Terry's spirits soared as the captain led him back to the chaplain's office. After talking together for a few minutes, the captain reached into his desk and withdrew a sheet of letterhead stationery. "Any time you need me, I'm here for you. Now, let's see. You'll need an official letter in order to attend Sabbath services." He wrote out the required information. "There. That should do it." He handed the letter to Terry, stood up, and shook the young cadet's hand. "Be looking forward to seeing you in church tomorrow."

Terry rode a wave of euphoria out of the church building and back to his barracks. His mother had been encouraging him to make friends with other Christians, and she'd been right. Yes, he thought, being with fellow believers will make things much easier. His eagerness to attend the Sabbath services carried him throughout the rest of the day. The next morning, he presented the chaplain's letter to Sergeant Collier.

Chapter Six

"Look at this!" Sergeant Collier shouted, waving the letter under Terry's nose. "One week, and you're already using your religion to get out of something, aren't you, slick?" The sergeant's upper lip curled into a familiar sneer. "Go on." He waved his arm in disgust. "Get out of my sight."

Terry grabbed his Bible and headed out the door. "Oh, Lord, now I've really got the man down on me. I don't know how much longer I can take this."

The church service provided the release Terry needed from the stress he'd been under. The few Seventh-day Adventists on the air force base met with the Adventist chaplain in a small room off the main chapel. They sang junior camp choruses as well as the old favorites. After the chaplain presented a short worship talk, the group talked with one another. As much as he enjoyed getting acquainted with other Adventists, he treasured the free copies of literature available. Copies of *Insight*, *Adventist Review*, *Guide*, *Listen*, and *Message* evoked memories of Sabbath afternoons at home.

"I'm so glad to see you could make it, Airman Johnson." The chaplain shook his hand vigorously as Terry prepared to leave. "I hope I'll see you here every Sabbath during your basic training."

"Oh, I'll be here," Terry replied, thinking of his training instructor's remarks. Under his breath he added, "As long as I'm still a member of the air force, anyway."

A picture of his mother flashed through his mind as he

walked down the front steps of the military chapel. She'd be so disappointed if he quit, but what else could he do? She'll understand, he reasoned as he made his way back to his barracks.

Staff Sergeant Collier didn't say anything about Terry's church attendance during the rest of the weekend. Fear coursed through Terry's mind as he let the hot spray from the shower pelt his back and neck on Monday morning. He knew it was only a matter of time before he felt the T.I.'s wrath. He turned off the faucet and reached for his towel. Yet, in the back of his mind, Terry could hear his mother's parting words. "No matter how bad things get, Jesus will see you through."

Breakfast and morning inspection passed without incident. The Texas sun already blistered the pavement in front of the barracks by the time the flight lined up for the marching practice.

"Slick, here." The sergeant shoved a canteen of water into Terry's hand. "You're road monitor today."

Whenever the recruits marched to an appointment, one person would run ahead of the fifty-man flight unit to the next traffic light and block traffic while the flight marched by. Then the same man would have to leap ahead of the flight in order to block traffic at the second light by the time the troops reached the corner. He would do this until the flight unit reached its destination. Usually, the staff sergeant divided the task of road monitor among several cadets, since the job took a high degree of stamina. The road monitor carried a full canteen of water in case he collapsed from exhaustion. The staff sergeant carried a container of smelling salts in case the water didn't work.

The young cadet waited for the sergeant to announce who the other road monitor would be. Instead, the sergeant ordered the flight to move out. "Get moving, Johnson. At the next corner, block the traffic to the left."

Terry set off on a run. The canteen jangled from his belt to the cadence of his stride. It felt good running in the morning air. When he joined the air force, he decided to cut out eating meat and fat products. In one week's time he could feel a difference physically and mentally. He found himself completing the required morning run with energy to spare, while most of the other exhausted cadets panted beside the road. A few of his friends noticed how strong Terry was becoming and opted for a vegetarian diet also, secretly referring to themselves as Daniel, Shadrach, Meshach, and Abednego.

Sprinting down the highway, Terry established an easy gait. At each intersection, he extended his arms as the troops marched by, a broad smile wreathing his face.

The sergeant, his eyebrows knitted in confusion, marched past the smiling cadet. When the last man had passed, the staff sergeant shouted again, "Block the traffic on the right." Intersection after intersection he met the same smiling, enthusiastic cadet. Mile after mile, the rest of the men began to droop. Even the sergeant showed signs of wear. The officer, shaking his head in amazement, thought the man should be flat on his back, panting for air; instead he looks as fresh as he did at the beginning of the run. When the sergeant and his men stumbled into the barracks, they were greeted by Terry's broad smile.

"Here, sir." He handed the sergeant the empty canteen, carefully cleaned and polished to a brilliant shine. Stunned, Collier stared at the canteen, then at the smiling cadet. The sergeant mumbled a few unintelligible words and retreated to his quarters.

Sergeant Collier enlisted the unit's other training instructors to mount his next attack in the cafeteria, or mess hall. The mess hall accommodated the entire squadron of 1,000 men at one time. Each training instructor was in charge of fifty men. Staff Sergeant Collier had been assigned to two flights simultaneously—100 men.

One glance at the "snake pit," a long table set back from the rest of the tables, where the training instructors drank coffee and smoked, assured Terry that of all the training instructors to whom he could have been assigned, Staff Sergeant Collier stood out as the tallest and the toughest—one lean, muscular, mean machine of a man, even among his peers. He emitted an attitude of cold, hard steel. Above the snake pit hung the squadron symbol and the flight symbol. Within the squadron symbol was the motto, "Lead, follow, or get out of the way." The instructors scrutinized the cadets to be certain all of the military rules for ordering and for eating their meals were observed. As for the cadets, their eyes could never stray toward the snake pit.

Unaware of Collier's latest plans, Terry stepped into the cafeteria line, placed his tray on the serving rollers, and ordered mashed potatoes without gravy and a serving of mixed vegetables. He then proceeded to the first empty table, where he waited, according to proper military procedure, for the next three airmen to join him. When the last cadet arrived with his food and gave the signal, the four men placed their trays on the table, pulled out their chairs, and sat down. As usual, Terry would choose most of his meal from the cafeteria's well-supplied salad bar.

Terry had just sat down and adjusted his chair when he heard his training instructor bawl from across the room, "Johnson, you're taking too long. Hurry it up and get your salad." Terry leaped to his feet as did one of the other cadets at his table. Along with the rule that he wasn't allowed to carry on a conversation at the table, an airman couldn't go alone to the salad bar. He must take another airman with him. This regulation was to promote teamwork among the new recruits.

Sergeant Collier knew about Terry's food preferences. "Hurry it up, Johnson. I'm going to give you a minute to get your salad and sit down." The other T.I.'s snickered as Terry rushed past the snake pit and over to the salad bar. He could feel the sympathetic glances of the other cadets in the room as he stacked a serving of lettuce onto his plate and reached for the tongs resting in the bowl of cherry tomatoes. He placed the vegetables on his plate and glanced over his shoulder at the training instructor. In his nervousness, Terry stepped behind the bar in order to reach the fruit bowl.

Again he heard the hated voice of his training instructor. "Johnson, what are you doing? Do you think this is Wendy's or something?" The nervous snickers of his fellow cadets and the

loud guffaws of the other training instructors followed. Terry's
buddies stared down at their food, knowing their friend was
once again in trouble.

"You think you can come in here and just help yourself,
huh? Come over here, flyboy." The sergeant motioned for him
to approach the snake pit. "Bring your tray over here!" The
tray rattled in Terry's hands as he approached the long table
of grinning sergeants.

"Oh, Lord." Terry stared up at the squadron symbol above
the table. "Help me have a positive attitude now."

The sergeant bent over the table, looking down into the
cadet's face and yelling at the top of his lungs. His words
vibrated against Terry's flushed face. "Don't you ever go behind the salad bar again!"

Shaking with fear, Terry gulped. "OK, sir." The moment the
two words escaped his mouth, Terry cringed in terror.

"OK? OK? What did you say, slick?" The room grew silent.
Thousands of eyes watched as the staff sergeant pulled himself to his full six-foot-six height, then strode around the
twenty-foot-long table to where the errant cadet stood rooted
like a noxious weed. The sergeant leaned forward, his chin
jutting out, and anger flashing from his icy blue eyes. "Not
yes, sir or no, sir, but OK, sir?"

Fluster beyond reason, Terry sat his tray on the officers'
table and snapped to attention.

"What! Did you put your tray on our table? Don't you know
you're not supposed to do that?" The sergeant leaned closer
into the young man's face, the rim of his Smokey-bear hat
touching Terry's forehead. "Do you understand me, slick?"

"O-o-o-K sir!" Instantly Terry recognized he'd done it again.
His eyes widened in horror.

Incredulous disbelief flooded the sergeant's face. "What did
you say?" A second training instructor walked around the
table to where the two men stood nose to nose. Sergeant
Collier slapped his own forehead in amazement, then turned
to the second sergeant. "Did I really hear him say that?"

"You sure did." The second sergeant glared and nodded.

A third training instructor moved in until the rims of all

three men's hats touched Terry's head, one at each ear, and with Staff Sergeant Collier's in front. The men screamed so loudly at the trembling airman that he couldn't make any sense out of what they were saying. Run! Run! his brain shouted to his body. I've got to get out of here. Muscles in his legs tightened in preparation for retreat. Instinctively he backed away.

"Are you trying to walk away when a T.I. is talking to you, flyboy?" Collier charged. A fourth instructor stepped up behind Terry, barring his only path of escape.

While the four training instructors yelled, Terry prayed. "Oh, Lord, I'm through. This is it. I know I'm finished." The verbal attack continued until he thought he would go out of his mind. "I can't believe You're allowing this to happen, Lord. I'm trying to eat right. If I'd eaten the regular food, this never would have happened. Lord, help me!"

After ten minutes of incessant bombardment, the training instructors turned and walked away, not because they'd run out of insults but because they couldn't contain their laughter any longer. Tears streamed down their faces as they stumbled back to their seats in the snake pit.

As he picked up his tray and hurried to his table, the dishes clattered together like stacked china in a major earthquake. His stomach churned, his appetite now buried somewhere beneath the rubble of his devastated military career.

Terry choked back both the unwelcome tears in his eyes and the acid rising in his throat. He stared at his uneaten meal until the other men at his table had finished their meals. Only then would he be allowed to leave the cafeteria. Finally, when he was free to go, Terry stumbled out of the mess hall into the stifling heat of the day.

Chapter Seven

Terry rushed out of the cafeteria, past a maze of sympathetic and jeering faces. He bounded up the stairs to his barracks, ran to his locker, and grabbed his Bible. Anger, humiliation, and frustration rumbled inside him like Mt. St. Helens's burning lava. He had to get off by himself. If he didn't, he'd spew out his fury on everybody. He slammed the locker door shut and immediately sensed someone standing nearby.

One of the cadets he'd not really gotten to know yet placed his hand on Terry's shoulder. "Tough luck, Johnson."

"Thanks, man," Terry muttered, eager to escape from everyone. "Hey, uh—"

"How did you keep from popping that guy one—right in the nose. I would have."

Terry smiled at his fellow cadet. "I can't say the idea didn't cross my mind."

"I don't know why you put up with the hassle. I would have been on the first flight home long ago."

"I've considered that too," Terry admitted.

"You're a whole lot stronger than I would be."

Terry shook his head. "It's not me; it's Jesus working in me."

The other cadet shook his head. "I guess I just don't understand."

Terry took a deep breath and realized he couldn't walk away from the man. He opened his Bible. "Well, it's like

40

this . . ." The two men talked for some time about God and His love for them. As the other cadets returned to the barracks, Terry invited the airman to join their Bible-study group. When the airman agreed, Terry strode over to his locker and reached inside. "Here's a book we've been reading, along with the Bible, of course."

Only one copy of *Steps to Christ* left. Ten—just enough for each of us. How did Mom know? he thought. Terry's public humiliation encouraged, instead of discouraged, the men's attendance at the Wednesday-night Bible-study/rap session he'd started.

On the third Friday morning of basic training, Terry stood beside his bunk folding his clean laundry when he heard the sergeant call his name. "Johnson, I want to see you in my office immediately." When Terry glanced around, Sergeant Collier had already reentered his office.

Terry's mind somersaulted through the events of the previous week, trying to remember what major infractions he might have unwittingly committed. Other than having messed up again on the marching field, he couldn't think of anything. Being called into the training instructor's office meant serious trouble. Terry walked with a stiff, disjointed gait into the office. He stepped over the threshold and saluted. His back stiffened even more when the sergeant walked behind him and butted the door closed. Staff Sergeant Collier only closed the office door when a cadet was being dismissed from the service.

Collier rounded the desk and sat down. "Forget the military, Johnson. At ease. Take a seat. We're just going to talk." The sergeant had the personality of a stun gun.

All the "at ease" commands in the U.S. military could not have relaxed Terry's churning stomach and fisted hands as he obeyed the sergeant's order. He drew his mouth into a pinched seam.

"Johnson, I have to confess to you that I have done everything I could possibly do to get rid of you during these last three weeks. I wouldn't blame you if you walked right down those stairs and reported me. What is it?" The officer paused as if choosing his words with great care. "How can you stay so

#%@# happy all the time? What's your secret?"

Stunned, Terry's jaw dropped open, and his eyes bugged out in wonder. *Does he really want to know? He won't like my answer . . .*

"Tell me, Johnson. I made your life miserable. How do you do it?"

Now it was Terry's turn to weigh his words carefully. "Oh, Father," he prayed silently before speaking, "put the right words into my mouth." With slow deliberation, he explained his newfound faith in God. He told the sergeant how God had increased his strength and patience equal to the officer's attacks. Staff Sergeant Collier leaned back in his chair and listened.

"Johnson, I thought I'd never say this about anybody, but you're for real. I can't believe it, but you're for real—a real Christian." He shook his head and pursed his lips. "I broke all the rules in my attempt to destroy you. I shouldn't be telling you this, but you could get me in a lot of trouble, you know. I had no right to harass you, especially about your religion." The man sighed. "In the face of every attack, you refused to lose your cool. I was hoping to get you so angry you'd either mouth off or take a swing at me, and I would have an excuse to send you packing. Worst of all," he pounded his fist on the desktop, "I can't help but like both you and your attitude."

Terry stared at his training instructor—the man who hated even the mention of religion. He never would have believed it possible.

The sergeant continued. "I'm going to give you a special assignment. I want to make you a chaplain guide during the rest of your basic training program. Your sole responsibility is to be a chaplain to the men of this flight. Encourage them to attend church services. Listen to their gripes and their problems." The sergeant leaned forward in his chair and peered across the desk at Terry. "Do your regular work; don't lay off, and don't tell anybody. I could get in trouble for this. If you're this positive and you can get the rest of the troops as positive, we can have an honor flight."

The man's honesty stunned Terry. Here was a chance to get

even. The old Terry would have leaped at the chance to get even with the sergeant who'd caused him so much grief. Getting him in trouble for the last three weeks of torment would feel so good. Then he remembered Elder Matula, his spiritual mentor. Terry had always thought of his Bible teacher as the genuine article, but himself? Never. Yet, that's what Sergeant Collier had called him, the real thing. Getting even wasn't the answer.

Terry knew how important the competition among the flights to win the honors as the top flight was to the training instructors. He discovered that Collier was eager to prove himself, being the newest of all the training instructors. He also knew that Sergeant Collier's image as a tough T.I. had suffered because of the religious cadet from the last flight he'd trained. That explained why he'd pushed Terry so hard.

"If I could just get the rest of the troops to have your good attitude and be as positive . . . if it's your Christ who's doing this to you, I could win honor flight."

Terry knew his answer before the man finished speaking. How could he turn down such an opportunity? "All right, sir, I'll be glad to be the flight's chaplain guide. What exactly will be my responsibilities?"

The sergeant thought for a moment. "I want you, first, as I said previously, to get the men to church each week. You'll be in charge of the flight all day Sunday. Make yourself available to the men for spiritual counseling." When he finished spelling out Terry's assignment, the training instructor reached in his desk drawer and pulled out a chaplain guide name tag and handed it to Terry. "You'll need to wear this whenever you march the men to their church services." Then Collier ran his fingers over his crew cut. "I can't believe I'm doing this. Me? Fostering religion?"

Terry couldn't believe his good fortune, either. Witnessing openly to the cadets in his barracks was more than he'd ever imagined. He knew God could do miracles, but change an embittered air force sergeant's heart in front of his peers and 1,000 cadets?

The change in Staff Sergeant Collier was subtle. While he

stopped singling Terry out for ridicule, he avoided contact with the young airman as much as possible. Terry knew the sergeant felt uncertain whether he should have trusted him with such a damaging admission. As the days passed, Collier relaxed his guard.

A rumor scuttling through camp made Terry nervous. The air force was eager to fill a shortage of trainees at the police academy. When he enlisted, he purposely indicated his first choice of going to chaplain school to train as a chaplain's assistant. What if the military switched his orders and assigned him to the police academy? Hadn't he told the air force recruiter back in Portland that he couldn't bear arms? Well, God has been in control of my life this far, Terry reasoned, He won't desert me now.

To be certain, Terry asked for and received permission to go to the base learning center to check that his assignment to chaplain school was in order.

The senior airman behind the desk shrugged off Terry's questions. "I wouldn't worry about it. I'm sure you're all set for chaplain's school." Terry left the learning center confident of his future. Within a few days he'd begin doing what he'd joined the military to do.

Chapter Eight

Terry immersed himself in the final weeks of his appointment as chaplain guide. The men of the squadron came to him regularly for advice. Rick eyed Terry's apparent success with disdain. Anytime Terry or one of the ten airmen who attended the Wednesday night Bible-study group made a mistake, Rick leaped at the opportunity to ridicule. "I thought you Christians didn't do things like that!"

Rick continued to probe for weak points in Terry's spiritual armor. Instead of discouraging Terry, Rick's attacks reminded him that he needed to continue searching for biblical answers for what he believed. While Terry never preached Adventism unless challenged directly, the men knew where Terry stood by his consistent lifestyle.

On the Monday before graduation from basic training, Terry asked to speak with Staff Sergeant Collier. "Sir, my mother is coming down from Oregon next weekend to the graduation exercises. My stepdad works for Amtrak, so she gets to travel for free on standby. And, well, I need to make arrangements for her stay."

The sergeant beamed with pleasure. Both Terry and the sergeant knew that assigning Terry as chaplain guide had been the best move the training instructor had made in a long time. Because of Terry's positive attitude and concern for the men, only four out of the original fifty men didn't stay throughout the entire basic training program. Forty of the forty-six remaining in the squadron had attended either their own churches on Sunday or Terry's on Saturday at least once during the five weeks of basic training.

"Don't you worry. I'll take care of everything, son. Is there anything else?"

Terry glanced down at the shiny gray tile on the floor, then back at the sergeant. "Yes, sir, one more thing. I don't know if you can help me or not, and I know this is highly irregular, but I need an advance on the two hundred dollars I will receive after I finish basic training."

"Oh?"

"I told you how my mother will be traveling standby on Amtrak. Well, I'd really like to send her back to Portland after the graduation exercises on a plane instead."

The sergeant picked up a pencil and tapped it against the desktop. "Are you telling me, son, that you plan to use your bonus money to buy your mom a plane ticket? Aren't you going to take it and blow it on a good time in town? You have been cooped up on base without wine or women for over a month now."

Terry cleared his throat. "It's a long trip to Oregon, and there's no guaranteeing she can get a seat when she's ready to leave. You gotta understand, my mom is one special lady."

"She must be." Staff Sergeant Collier slowly rose from his desk. "Airman, you never cease to amaze me." He circled the desk and went to the inner office door. "Henderson," he called to the first sergeant at work in the next office, "you gotta hear this. You'll never believe it." Collier told the first sergeant of Terry's request. As he spoke, the first sergeant peered around Staff Sergeant Collier's shoulder at Terry and shook his head.

"This is a first!" Henderson admitted. "I gotta tell the unit commander this one. You're really serious?"

Fearful he'd made himself look stupid again, Terry nodded and mumbled an unintelligible, "Yes, sir."

The unit commander reacted with the same disbelief. "I can't believe you'd do this for your mother. Of course we'll get you your advance, Airman Johnson."

Terry's mother arrived a week before the graduation exercises. The sergeant had made all the arrangements for her to stay at the guest quarters on base.

On Sabbath morning, Terry planned to take her to the base chapel. He gave his uniform dress shoes one last shine, then straightened. He glanced down at his watch. Eight thirty-five, time to pick up his mother to take her to church.

"Johnson." Sergeant Collier strode out of his office and called across the room to Terry. "Are you preparing to leave for church?"

"Yes, sir. My mother's waiting for me now."

"Wonderful woman, that mother of yours." The sergeant jutted his chin and narrowed his eyes as if he wanted to say more. "And she's mighty proud of you, son."

"Thank you, sir." Terry cocked his head to one side, uncertain as to what he should do or say next. He glanced nervously at his watch, then back at the sergeant.

"About time to go?" Sergeant Collier's scowl deepened.

"Yes, sir."

The sergeant cleared his throat. "Uh . . . mind if I join you and your mother, Johnson?"

Terry's mouth dropped open; his eyes widened. Never in his wildest imagination could he have foreseen the sergeant's request. "Join us, sir?"

"Well, yes, go to church with you this morning—if you don't mind, that is."

"Oh, no, of course not. I'd be delighted to have you along. Mom would too." Terry grabbed the shoe-shine cloth and placed it back in his locker. "Ready to go?"

During the final weeks of basic training, Terry had had little time to talk with the sergeant about spiritual matters. Yet he had noted the changes. Even the other men in the flight commented that the staff sergeant's words had become less cutting than previously.

The sergeant walked with Terry to the guest quarters. If Terry's mother was surprised to see Staff Sergeant Collier along, she didn't show it. She treated the burly sergeant as if he were another of her boys.

Cool morning breezes accompanied them on their walk to the base chapel. As they stepped inside, the sergeant admitted, "It's been a good thirteen years since I last attended church, you know. My wife, or I should say, my former wife, thought a lot of her religion."

They strode down the hall to the side room where the little congregation met each week. Sabbath School had already begun. They had just sat down when Staff Sergeant Collier gasped. "That's Gonzales," he whispered to Terry.

"Excuse me?"

"The man behind the pulpit is Master Sergeant Gonzales, the man who trained me to be a training instructor. I didn't know he was a Seventh-day Adventist."

Terry smiled to himself. Of all the coincidences . . .

After the services, Staff Sergeant Collier introduced Terry and his mother to his former mentor, Master Sergeant Gonzales.

"Well," Gonzales exclaimed. "I am sure glad to see you attending church, Collier. When did you become interested in Adventism?"

Staff Sergeant Collier glanced at Terry, then at the other man. "It's a long story, sir."

"I'd be interested in hearing it." The man shook Collier's hand and grinned at Terry. "Stop by my office sometime."

All the way back to the barracks, the sergeant marveled over meeting Gonzales at the church. "I always knew there was something different about him, but I never knew what. How could I have missed it?"

Throughout the week before graduation, the airmen practiced marching long hours each day. On the eve of graduation, Terry still found himself turning left when he should turn right or falling out of step on the parade ground. At the graduation, each flight would demonstrate their marching skills before the four, one-thousand member squadrons. The flight's performance on the parade ground was crucial to the group's final score and the possibility of winning the honor ribbon of the squadron. Not only did the ribbon produce pride in the members of the flight for their outstanding achievement, but it also allowed them special recognition. Their flight would get to go first during every activity throughout the last week of training after the graduation exercises. If other flights were waiting in line to process their paperwork, when the honor flight arrived, the first flight in line would have to relinquish their place to the honor flight. The staff sergeant received the respect of the other training instructors and a commendation on his permanent military record.

The sun had set before Staff Sergeant Collier called the men into a huddle to discuss the next day's activities. "OK, men, what can we do to make the flight really shine? We want to look the best we can when we march before the brass tomorrow."

One of Terry's friends laughed and said, "Don't let Gomer march." Terry laughed along with the other cadets.

"That's not such a bad idea." The sergeant eyed Terry for a few seconds. "I need to appoint one of you to do dorm watch during the graduation exercises. It might as well be Terry. All in favor?" Forty-five hands shot into the air. "The vote is unanimous. Terry, you've been elected to watch the dorm tomorrow."

The next morning Terry didn't have time to tell his mother he wasn't marching. However, with more than 4,000 uniformed men marching, she couldn't tell one cadet from the other, even her own son.

Terry sat guarding the door and reading his Bible, when Jeff and Tom bounded into the barracks. "We won, Johnson. We won!" Jeff ran to Terry and pounded him on the back.

"Yeah," Tom added, "and we couldn't have done it without you."

Jeff pounded Terry on the shoulder and snorted. "Or *with* you, for that matter."

"Huh? I don't understand."

Tom explained. "The points that put us over the top were from the unusually high number of our men attending church, for which you deserve the credit."

Jeff continued. "And we couldn't have won with you if you'd marched today. So, see, we couldn't have the honor flight without you, and we couldn't have won it with you."

Chapter Nine

Terry strolled across the base toward his barracks. Seeing his mother off at the airport left him feeling terribly alone once more. Yet, an eager anticipation for the future lay submerged beneath the surface of his loneliness. One more week of basic training, and he would finally begin training for his real mission. The more he thought about how God had worked everything out for him, the lighter his step grew. He began whistling the melody to his favorite hymn, "Amazing Grace."

After breakfast on Monday morning, as the members of his flight packed their belongings to leave, Terry sought out Staff Sergeant Collier to say goodbye. "Airman Johnson, it's been a pleasure knowing you. You've taught me a lot. Sorry about the rough beginning . . ."

Terry gazed at his training instructor for a moment, marveling at the subtle changes he'd seen during the last few weeks of basic training. "Sir, I guess I can't exactly say it's been a pleasure, at least not all of it, anyway, but I have to admit that you helped me grow up a lot, and I will never forget it."

This was the last time the flight would be together. From here the men would fly to air force training centers in different parts of the United States. The men who had studied together every Wednesday night pledged to keep in contact with one another and with their newfound friend, Jesus Christ. Terry reminded them that if they lost contact on this earth, they could, if faithful, attend a grand reunion in heaven.

Jeff pounded Terry on the back. "I'm gonna miss ya, Gomer, old buddy."

Terry's eyes misted. "I'll miss you too. Good luck, man."

The air crackled with tension and excitement as the men assembled on the parade ground. The day promised to be another sweltering example of summer in Texas. Terry wiped his brow and dropped his duffle bag in front of him. An officer ordered them to "fall in," then called them to attention. "I will read off your social security number, then the bus you should board for the drive to the airport for your respective flights."

When Terry heard his number called, he climbed aboard the bus indicated and found a seat. In a short time, the buses pulled out. Terry looked about at the large number of cadets on his bus. He couldn't believe his eyes. "All of these men are going to the assistant chaplain training school?"

Near the main entrance to the base, when some of the buses peeled off to the left toward the guard station, Terry's bus, as well as a number of others behind it, turned right. They rode for a short time through a thickly wooded area, never leaving the base. The buses broke into a clearing and stopped in front of a large gray building. The sign out front read "United States Air Force Police Academy."

Terry jolted to attention. "Police academy? There must be some mistake."

After the last bus emptied its passengers, a sergeant ordered the 300 men to line up. "When I read your Social Security number, raise your hand. You will be issued your military-regulation M-16 rifle."

Terry only half-heard the rest of the sergeant's speech. There must be some mistake, he assured himself. Maybe I'm to be a chaplain guide to this group during my training to become an assistant chaplain.

When the sergeant called out Terry's Social Security number, Terry raised his hand. The sergeant shoved a rifle at the startled airman, "Excuse me, but where's my Bible? I'm going to be an assistant to a chaplain."

Laughter exploded up and down the line. The sergeant ran his gaze along the list of Social Security numbers on his check sheet. "What? What do you mean, Bible? You're in the police academy, airman."

"But you see, I won't need a rifle. I was assigned to assist the chaplain here."

Another snicker passed through the group, along with a few groans. No one wanted to stand in the heat any longer than necessary, least of all the sergeant in charge. "Look, I don't know anything about a Bible or a chaplain's assistant. Take your rifle." He dropped the gun into Terry's arms. "Here's the rifle number."

"But—" Terry stared at the weapon with horror. The only gun he'd ever touched was a friend's .22 rifle when he was a kid.

The man sighed. "Just take the M-16, Airman Johnson, and we'll send you to talk with someone after we finish the paperwork."

With the rifles distributed, Terry headed in the direction of his new barracks.

"Hey, Johnson," a familiar voice called from behind. "Are you still giving the brass fits and commotions?"

At the sound of his name, Terry whirled about. Jeff and Tom ran toward him. "Imagine this, we're together again. The three musketeers."

"Well, for now, anyway," Terry reminded. "Obviously I can't stay in the police academy. I'm a conscientious objector. I can't bear arms."

Tom heaved his duffle onto his shoulder. "Aw, don't worry, Johnson, the military will work it all out. Let's go find our bunks and get out of these dress blues."

Terry shook his head and hurried to keep up with his two friends. "I hope so."

While Terry watched, the other two unloaded their gear and organized their lockers. He didn't think it made much sense to unpack his duffle bag since he'd probably be leaving in a couple of hours, once the brass discovered their error.

"Airman Johnson." The sergeant in charge of his barracks called his name. "Report to the administration building immediately."

"See guys." Terry stood up. "I told you they'd get it all straightened out right away."

Terry hurried to the administration office. He gave the clerk his name.

The senior airman looked up from his computer. "He's waiting for you. You may go right in."

Once in the staff sergeant's office, Terry explained his problem. "So you see, when I enlisted, I did so with the understanding that I would be sent to chaplain school. As I'm a conscientious objector, police academy would be the last place I would want to be."

The staff sergeant listened, then turned to his computer and called up Terry's file. "Hmm, according to our records, there's no mention of your being a CO." Terry could feel the sweat beading on his forehead as the staff sergeant read through his entire file. "You have a great recommendation from your training instructor." He glanced up at Terry, then back at the computer screen, "Hmmm, why don't you stay one week and do the best you can while I do some checking. Then we'll try to ship you off to the right place."

Lackland Air Force Base
San Antonio, Texas
Summer 1985

Chapter Ten

Terry grabbed his M-16 and headed back to the barracks after an afternoon of target practice. An entire week had passed—a week of instruction on the use of weapons he knew he could never bring himself to fire against another human being. He dropped his rifle off at the barracks and headed for the administration building. Surely the air force would have cut his new assignment by now.

He informed the clerk of his need to see the staff sergeant once again. The clerk informed the staff sergeant on the intercom and told Terry to go right in. The staff sergeant attempted to explain the mix-up with his orders as a computer error. "Now, I'm afraid it's too late. There are no openings in the chaplain's assistant training program at this point. As I see it, Airman Johnson, you have two choices; either stay and complete your training at the police academy or go home."

"That's it, sir?"

The staff sergeant leaned back in his desk chair and raised his hands in defeat. "That's it."

Terry couldn't believe it. All the weeks of basic training for nothing? God had done so much for him. It isn't all over, he thought, not now, not like this. "I'd like to think about it, sir, over the weekend, if I may."

Desperate for answers or at least an intelligent ear, he decided to call home. The last rays of sunlight disappeared over the horizon when Terry dropped the coins into the pay phone outside the barracks. "Mom? That you? Yeah, this is Terry."

Immediately his mother sensed something was wrong from the tone of her son's voice and told him so. Tears glistened in Terry's eyes as he explained his plight. "What should I do? Quit? What other choice do I have?" When she didn't answer immediately, he continued. "Maybe I should come home and enroll in Walla Walla College like I planned before I enlisted. Maybe that's what God wanted all the time." Even Terry could hear the distinctive ring of homesickness in his words.

"Son, I've been praying about this and feel it's God's will for you to stay. I don't think the Lord is done with you yet." His mother's answer came through strong and confident. His heart ached at the sound of her voice. "Stick it out as long as you can. Pray about it before you make any hasty changes."

That's not what I want to hear, Terry thought. He scuffed the toe of his boot in the sand outside the door of the phone booth. "Thanks, Mom. I know you'll be praying for me that I'll do the right thing."

"So will the people at the Sharon Church," she reminded.

When Terry hung up the receiver, he felt hollow, empty, desolate. He gazed at the evening sky. Everything and everyone he loved seemed to be millions of miles away, as far as the stars appearing overhead. He made his way back to the barracks and readied himself for bed. As he stretched out beneath the military-issue sheet and blanket, he tried to fall asleep, but sleep refused to come.

Since joining the air force, his life had become one gigantic roller coaster full of unexpected dips, mountains, twists, and turns. He had carried out his commission of company morale officer with unbridled enthusiasm. Cadets with marital problems had come to him for advice. Cadets with other personal and family problems did the same. Already, he was becoming known as "that Christian guy" in his new flight. While it seemed that God was in control of his life, he wrestled with questions and doubts. Why would God put me in the security police? The only place in the air force that requires one to carry weapons, he thought. "The only place, Lord! Why?"

The next morning he finished breakfast and strode across the base to the chapel. He entered the cool confines of the sanctuary and walked to the side room where the Sabbath services were held. He enjoyed getting there before the others and spending time reading the latest issues of *Insight*, *Signs*, and *Message* magazines. This Sabbath, the magazines produced a major case of homesickness instead of comfort.

He'd just finished the lead article in *Insight* magazine when Gail, an Adventist woman involved in the officer's training program, who'd graduated from Oakwood College, entered the room. During the toughest weeks of his basic training, she'd been there to encourage him. The petite, effervescent woman shattered any preconceived notions he might have had of the typical military-type woman.

She crackled with energy as she pulled up a chair and started badgering him with questions. "So, tell me, how did it go this week? Are you all set? Where are they sending you?"

Terry shook his head.

"What? What? OK, spill it."

He explained all that had happened. "Now I don't know what to do."

"Oh, boy. I don't know what to tell you, Terry." Gail shook her head, then glanced toward the door. "Here's the chaplain. He'll know what to do."

Terry retold his story to the chaplain.

"Well," the chaplain shook his head, "you signed up. Either you go to the police academy, or you go home. I don't see any other choices."

Bill, a premed student from Loma Linda who'd entered the officer's training program to pay off student loans, joined the group. "And there's just nothing the air force is willing to do?"

"I guess not." Terry shook his head. "I talked with my mom last night. She thinks I should stick it out, that God wants me here for another reason."

The chaplain shrugged. "Only you can decide."

While they were speaking, a black, middle-aged gentleman in civilian clothes stepped into the room and sat down in the back row. He moved up next to Terry when the chaplain went to greet another worshiper. The stranger turned to Terry. "You look a little down, son. What's wrong?"

Terry told him his story. "I knew God wanted me here when He changed the sergeant's heart, but now, I just don't know."

The man frowned and shook his head slowly. "Whatever you do, don't get out now. God has a purpose for bringing you here. We need Christians in the military." He paused. "I've been in twenty-odd years, and I've had chances to witness and work with a lot of people whom I would never have met in any other capacity. Don't give up, whatever you do; don't give up."

Terry studied the man's face. "You know, you're the first person, outside of my mother, who has encouraged me to stick with it."

The man smiled, stood up, and shook Terry's hand. "Here's my card. If you have any problems, give me a call. Just tell your T.I. you need to call a friend."

"Thanks." Terry took the card and slipped it into his pocket.

The stranger clapped a hand on Terry's shoulder. "Keep up your spirits, son. You'll make it." Terry watched the man walk away and searched his memory as to where he'd seen him before. Probably working in the chow line at the cafeteria or something, he thought.

Back at the barracks that evening, Terry emptied the pockets of his dress uniform for the once-a-week trip to the dry cleaners. The card fell out on the bed. He picked it up and read it. "Colonel Leonard Johnson." Colonel? Terry read the card again. No doubt about it. The stranger was a colonel. Terry withered in horror. I dumped my problems on a colonel? he thought. Maybe the guy wasn't for real. Maybe the card wasn't really his.

Curious, Terry arranged to visit the chaplain and ask him about the stranger he'd talked with at the church service. "Sure, it was Colonel Leonard Johnson. He's one of the air force's only flying doctors and an Adventist, I might add. I understand he returned to his base in Florida this week."

On the way back to his barracks, Terry gave in. "OK, Lord, I'm in Your hands. It's Your move."

Chapter Eleven

Terry ran a sweaty hand along the smooth surface of the M-16's barrel and watched as one after another of the police academy cadets stepped up to the firing platform and aimed down a fairway at a distant bull's-eye.

"This is not why I joined the air force," he mumbled as the weapons instructor, informally dubbed "red cap," called Terry's number. "I believe You are in control of my life, but I really don't belong here, Lord!"

Sweat beaded on Terry's brow, running in tiny rivulets down the sides of his face as he took his place on the shooting platform and leveled his rifle at the target. This was the qualifying heat for the M-16 rifle—the first of many weapons he would need to master in order to complete his training at the police academy. He held his breath as he fired a round of bullets, then stepped back into line. The countdown continued until all 100 men in the group had had a turn at acquiring their share of points on the target.

Terry had to admit that other than the actual weapons training, he hadn't found life at the police academy difficult. His reputation for not being able to march and his reputation as a Christian followed him. The nickname, Gomer, didn't prevent the men from coming to him with their problems. Since life at the academy was less rigid, some of his friends from basic training would come over to his barracks for their Wednesday-night Bible-study group. Considering everything, Terry felt satisfied with the way God was ironing out the wrinkles in his life.

He talked with a few of his friends while the men waited for the red cap to tally the points they'd scored on the shooting range. He squinted up at the searing Texas sun. Oh, for a few healthy clouds from the Northwest, he thought. One of his friends suggested they head to the PX after supper. "I'm in the mood for a giant root beer float."

After the weapons instructor collected the targets and totaled the scores, he called for the cadets to fall in. "Something has happened today that has never happened before, at least not since I've been at the academy. Today, one person in our group not only didn't make enough points to qualify but never even hit the target, once." Grins and snickers passed through the group.

Terry's thoughts mirrored the other ninety-nine cadets' thoughts—imagine not even coming close to the target.

The sergeant continued. "I can't believe this has happened, so I am going to do something I have never done before. First, I'm going to move the target a little closer; then I'm going to allow Airman Johnson to try again."

Me? Terry felt heat rising up his neck and into his face. Oh, no! As he stepped forward, he could hear the nickname, Gomer Pyle, passing from cadet to cadet. Knowing that many of them used it good-naturedly didn't lessen the sting. If he messed up once, what was to stop him from doing it again? he thought. The last thing he wanted to do was make a fool of himself a second time.

The news spread along the entire length of the firing range. Other training flights stopped their shooting practice session. More than 400 people gathered to view the situation. The sergeant reviewed the instructions on aiming and holding the rifle steady with Terry, then told him to try again. Only the incessant Texas wind broke the silence as Terry hefted the rifle to his shoulder, positioned the target in his sights, and fired a second round of bullets.

As the smoke settled, Terry removed the protective earphones from his head and placed them on the equipment stand. Then he and his audience waited as the training instructor stomped down the shooting range to tally Terry's new scores. The red cap returned, shaking his head. "I don't understand it. I just don't understand it. No one has ever missed the target that badly."

Terry's shoulders slumped forward. "I did just what you told me to do." Under his breath, he was praying, "Lord, I don't understand it. You wanted me here when I wanted to be elsewhere. I need Your help, now!"

The instructor removed his hat and wiped his brow. He flashed Terry a beleaguered look and rolled his muddy brown eyes at the growing number of observers. "I'd like to let you try a third time, son, but I could get into trouble if I did. Maybe . . ." He scowled, then strode over to a field telephone near the ammunitions shack.

Terry's friends gathered around him. "What are you going to do, Terry, if you flunk out?" Jeff asked, "I mean, you said you believed God placed you here in the police academy for a reason. What now?"

One of the men in his unit who scoffed at religion and at Terry's claim to Christianity added, "Yeah, you said your God is always with you. Well, where is your God now?"

Terry shook his head. He'd seen God's leading in so many ways since joining the air force, he couldn't lose faith now. He looked at the crowd of people gathered. Could God have set this up so I could witness to all these people today? Perhaps this really is my chance to bring honor to His name. He smiled to himself.

He looked at his friends and at the man who had cast doubt on his God. "Hey, I don't know what is happening, but I do know that God has a plan in all of this." Terry laughed self-consciously. "Maybe He intends to perform a miracle."

"From what I see," the doubter quipped, "it's going to take a mighty big one this time."

When the red cap returned, the men stepped back to let him through. "I talked to headquarters," he tipped his head toward the administration building behind them, "and got permission to move the target even closer and give you one more try."

Terry followed the training instructor's gaze toward the administration offices. People streamed from the building onto the lawn. Others hung out the windows. Still more filled the roadway to catch a glimpse of the cadet who couldn't hit the target, much less the bull's-eye.

The training instructor ordered his assistant to move the target twenty feet closer. "OK, Airman Johnson. Now concentrate on the target. Make the rifle an extension of your arm."

The tension grew as Terry loaded his rifle and strode up to the shooting platform. He took his time aiming, praying while he adjusted his sights. Then, in rapid succession, he fired off the round and set the weapon down to await the results. His friends flocked to his side in support. Instead, he tried to reassure them of his faith in God. "Don't worry, God's in control. He's never failed me before, and He's not going to fail me now."

Jeff shook his head. "Man, I hope you're right."

Terry clapped his hand on Jeff's back. "Hey, don't worry. It's God's reputation at stake, not mine." Jeff looked at Terry, then beyond into the somber face of the training instructor.

Terry felt a tap on his shoulder and turned. "I'm sorry. We've never had this happen before. You flunked."

Shock, humiliation, and frustration flooded through Terry. He couldn't believe it. God would never leave him hanging out to dry; He'd always come through for him. "What now?"

The sergeant turned to allow a second, higher-ranking sergeant pass sentence. "He'll have to go back a week and begin the program again with the new recruits. He'll have to go 'casual.'"

Casual? Terry's heart sank. Nothing could be more humiliating at the police academy than to have to enter casual training, a program for the cadets who couldn't qualify for their particular assignments. The training instructors used casual training as a threat over their flight members. The "casual" airmen were marked men. They were required to untuck their shirts and to wear a different type of hat to distinguish them from the regular cadets. They were assigned to work duty, cutting grass, painting buildings, general cleanup. Training instructors and regular cadets alike taunted the hapless men assigned to this probationary post. Those who still failed to qualify after doing time in the casual training program would be sent home.

The sergeant instructed Terry to pack up his gear and move to the barracks of the incoming flight of trainees. Mortified, Terry slung his rifle over his shoulder, hunched deeper into his shirt collar, and returned to his barracks. Along the way, his buddies tried to comfort him.

"There must be a reason, man," Tom reminded. "Remember how rough Collier was on you? God had reason in that, didn't He?"

Terry nodded and climbed the stairs to his flight room. His friends followed.

"Listen to him, Terry," Jeff admonished. "There must be a purpose in this. Don't lose faith in God now, not now that so many of your buddies have just found Him."

Terry looked at Tom. The image of Tom as he was when they'd met the first day of basic training surfaced in Terry's mind. Still wily and mouthy, the young street-hard punk with the major "attitude" had mellowed into a thoughtful, searching individual. No, Terry thought, Jeff is right, I can't lose faith. For Tom's sake, I can't blow it now.

Discouraged beyond consolation, Terry said goodbye to his friends and crossed the compound to his new barracks. His feet dragged; his heart ached. "In front of all those people, Lord . . . in front of all those people, I stood up for You. I vowed You wouldn't let me down!" He ground his teeth in anger. "How could You humiliate me in front of all those people after all I've done for You? How? How?"

Immediately after his outburst, Terry regretted his lack of faith. He now knew how Job must have felt sitting on his hill of ashes as well as David, on the run from his own son. Both men had done nothing more than be honest with God, and they'd been forgiven. "Father, I'm sorry, not for being honest with You, but for forgetting that You know the end from the beginning. You were mortified for me on the cross; how can I do less?"

Terry decided to do his best in spite of the demotion. When

training instructors passed and hollered insults like, "Hey, look at that slob over there. If he doesn't get his act together, we're gonna drum him out of the force," Terry would smile and continue working.

On Tuesday of Terry's first week on casual, the weapons training instructor called him to the shooting range and tested him again. Again he aimed and missed the target. Disappointed, Terry fought to maintain a good attitude. "Come back on Thursday, son."

On Thursday, the same thing happened. The red cap shook his head in disbelief. "I'm not supposed to do this, but come back next Tuesday."

Over the weekend, Terry pushed all thoughts of Tuesday from his mind. "Whatever will be, Lord," he prayed.

Tuesday arrived. Terry hurried to the shooting range to keep his appointment with the instructor. While he tried to maintain an outward cool, he couldn't keep the rush of adrenalin from raising his pulse rate. He moved through the steps of firing with a calm precision.

As Terry took off the safety earphones, the red cap ran down the field to the target with his clipboard. Terry watched the man return, noting the intense frown on his face. "Well, this time you did hit the target," the training instructor mumbled. "Unfortunately, your total isn't high enough. You lack five points to qualify."

Terry groaned. He pushed away the dark cloud of anger that tried to invade his mind.

The red cap tapped his pen against the clipboard as he studied Terry's scores. "Airman Johnson, I see something in you that the air force needs. So I'm gonna do something I've never done before. I'm gonna let you go ahead. You're only a few points off anyway." The weapons instructor hastily added five points to Terry's score and signed the qualification sheet.

"I-I-I b-b-but—"

"Johnson, you're dismissed."

"Yes, sir!" Terry snapped off a salute and ran.

Having been taken off casual, Terry was assigned to a new barracks. He tossed his belongings into his duffle bag and sprinted across the base to his new home. As he reached the front steps of the new building, he paused. Dark memories of Staff Sergeant Collier leaped into his mind. Nervous butterflies battered the walls of his stomach. He breathed a short prayer, squared his shoulders, and entered the building. Setting his gear down by the door, he walked over to the training instructor's office and knocked on the doorjamb. The door itself was open, and the T.I. stood with his back to the door searching for something in an open file drawer. The nameplate on the desk read Staff Sergeant Dan Edding. The man turned to face Terry.

"Sir," Terry began, "I was told to report to your flight. My name is Airman Terry Johnson."

The training instructor eyed him thoughtfully for a moment. When recognition hit, the man struggled to control the start of a smile. "You must be the guy I've been hearing about. Now let me get this straight. You took the M-16 qualifications test three times and never hit the target once?"

Terry flushed. "Yes, sir."

A smile teased the corners of the sergeant's mouth into a slow, easy smirk. "What were you doing, Airman Johnson, partying all night the night before?"

Like a splash of cold water, shock filled Terry's face. "Oh, no, sir. I don't party all night. I'm a Christian."

Staff Sergeant Edding knitted his brows and frowned.

Oh, no, Terry thought, not another Sergeant Collier story.

The man cocked his head to one side and lifted an eyebrow. "What denomination?"

Flooded with dread, Terry cleared his throat. "Seventh-day Adventist."

"Hmmm." The sergeant walked over to his desk chair and sat down. "Then you'll be wanting your Saturdays off, right?"

"Yes, sir." Terry's heart sank down to his regulation combat boots. "Not again, Lord," he prayed, "not again."

Chapter Twelve

"Well, Johnson." The man tapped his ballpoint pen against the desk pad. "I'll give you every Sabbath off." Sergeant Edding ran the length of the pen through his fingers a few times before he continued. " . . . seems your God worked a miracle in your behalf. Out of all the training instructors here at the academy, I'm the only practicing Christian." The man leaned back in his chair and grinned. "In fact, we have something else in common. According to your file, you're planning to be an SDA minister, while I'm studying to become a Nazarene preacher. Don't worry, I will take you to church if necessary."

Terry heaved a gigantic sigh of relief and broke into a wide grin. "Oh, sir, you don't know how happy that makes me feel. I had a rough time during basic training, and, well, I was afraid it was about to start all over again."

"It happens sometimes," the sergeant admitted. The two men talked about their experiences as Christians in the military. When Terry told him about the Wednesday-night Bible-study sessions, the sergeant broke into a wide grin. "On Friday nights I conduct a rap session/Bible-study thing here in the barracks. Would you be interested in combining our efforts? You can preach about whatever you want—no holds barred."

The cadet's eyes lighted up. "Oh, I'd like that, sir. I'll talk to the other guys in our group to be sure, but I'd really like that."

The sergeant stood up and shook Terry's hand. "Welcome aboard, airman. Why don't you go settle in."

Terry snapped to attention, saluted, and strode from the office. He found an empty bunk and sat down on the edge of the bed. As his emotions leveled off, he thought about the doubts he'd had on the shooting range and buried his face in his hands. "Oh, when will I learn to trust You with my life? When will I stop doubting You, Lord?"

Terry thrived on the Friday-night sessions, when he and the sergeant could exchange philosophies and ideas. Each week more of his peers joined the rap session instead of heading into town to the nearest bar, until the circle of ten grew to more than sixty, and they had to meet in the chapel. The men studied the four Gospels, starting with Matthew. When the subject of the Sabbath came up, Sergeant Edding gestured toward Terry. "Hey, this guy's the expert on the Sabbath. He can tell you about it."

Terry couldn't believe his good fortune. This is what I joined the military for, he admitted to himself as he shared the Sabbath truths with his friends.

While his spiritual life smoothed out, his military performance remained the same—horrible, in particular, his marching skills. He didn't fit in with the hard-driving, hard-drinking commando attitude of most of the other police academy cadets and instructors. Being called "preacher boy" became a badge of honor instead of an insult. The same was not true of his other nickname, Gomer Pyle.

The first day back on the shooting range, the weapons instructor took advantage of the fact that Terry was familiar with the M-16. "Preacher boy?" the red cap called good-naturedly.

Terry stepped forward and swallowed hard. The instructor might have confidence in Terry's advanced knowledge of the equipment, but Terry certainly didn't. He stared at the weapon with a distinct distrust.

The red cap gestured toward the shooting platform. "I want you to give the new cadets a demonstration on the proper use of the M-16 so they can get used to the sound. Just squeeze off three or four shots."

The sweat ran down the middle of his back as he stepped

up to the shooting block and slipped the safety earphones over his ears. Just once, he thought, just once I'd love to execute an order without making a fool of myself. He leveled the rifle up to his shoulder and pulled the trigger. In his anxiety, he failed to release the trigger. The splatter of open machine gun fire resounded across the shooting range like fireworks on the Fourth of July. The barrel of his gun turned fiery red as he emptied the entire magazine. Shaken by the violent barrage, Terry lowered his rifle and staggered back from the target area. He cast a silent plea toward the red cap. The weapon's instructor's mouth hung open in stunned silence. The new recruits stared in frozen horror.

Rattled, the instructor waved the recruits off. "You-you're dismissed for today."

News of the "preacher boy's" latest performance on the rifle range traveled throughout the camp. Good-natured joshing followed Terry wherever he went. While the red cap still used him as comic relief whenever possible, the instructor never asked him to demonstrate the M-16 rifle again.

Determined to master the required skills, Terry practiced and qualified his way through the list of the M-16 rifle, M-60 machine gun, and the M-203 grenade launcher. He surprised the weapons instructor by earning a ribbon for marksmanship with the M-60.

Other training instructors took advantage of Terry's previous knowledge of the skills and of his easygoing attitude. Part of their instruction included "smart team training." Like civilian SWAT teams, the air force teaches the techniques of surprise invasion into terrorist-held buildings and compounds to rescue potential hostages. The morning when the smart team instructor introduced rappeling down the side of a building on ropes, he waved Terry toward the roof of a three-story building.

"Preacher boy, go on up there and show us how it's done while I explain the process to the new men. This is used to rescue hostages in a terrorist situation."

The glass in the windows of the yellow brick building regularly used for this particular training routine had been replaced with lightweight sheets of plywood that would give when the airmen's feet touched it.

When Terry appeared in full gear on the roof building, the training instructor shouted through his bullhorn, "Now just rappel down and enter the building through the third window from the left. You got that?"

Terry peered down at the flight members assembled on the lawn below and gave the instructor a thumbs-up signal. On the instructor's command, Terry swung over the edge of the building like a hawk swooping toward its prey. As he plummeted toward his target, either a gust of wind or a miscalculation altered his descent. He realized it was too late to adjust for either as the solid yellow bricks zoomed toward his face. With a painful thunk, Terry smashed feet first, not into the wooden windows, but into the side of the building. He bounced off the wall and struck it again. The roar of laughter from below outweighed the sudden shock to the bottom of his feet.

Once the training instructor was certain Terry had sustained no permanent injuries, he joined in the laughter. No matter how much they might like and admire the young Christian, both the police academy instructors and his fellow cadets could see what Terry knew all along. He just didn't fit in with the commando image and lifestyle. As the end of the course loomed closer, Terry wrestled over his future. How could he possibly be assigned to guard a strategic military installation while in his heart he longed for a much different assignment? Occasionally he shared his concerns with the men in his Bible-study group.

"Don't worry, Terry," Sergeant Edding reminded. "God has worked everything out so far. Why should He stop now?"

Chapter Thirteen

One Friday, during the last few weeks of training, Jeff pulled Terry aside after their Bible study. "Have you heard about tryouts for the President's Honor Guard next week?"

"Yeah, Sergeant Edding mentioned it this morning at inspection." Terry fell into step beside his friend as they headed toward their respective barracks. "Boy, what an assignment! Are you going to try out?"

"Well, buddy," Jeff clapped his friend on the shoulder, "I was sort of hoping you'd come with me to give me courage. Of course, you don't stand a chance, but I'd sure like it if you'd go along and support me and pray for me."

Terry admitted to himself that his friend was being truthful, not malicious. He knew he really didn't stand a chance, not with his horrible marching record and weapons ratings. "Sure buddy, be glad to."

Try out for the President's Honor Guard? As good an airman as Jeff is, what chance does he really have of making it? Terry thought. Talk about reaching for the stars. The President's Honor Guard was the highest goal for any air force cadet. The scuttlebutt in the police academy claimed that only generals' kids or graduates of a military academy got in to the prestigious group. He knew that less than 3 percent of the entire air force ever got a chance to even see the Honor Guard in action. Terry couldn't blame Jeff for at least wanting to try. After serving in the President's Honor Guard, an airman could write his own ticket throughout the rest of his military career. Even in his wildest imagination, Terry held out no hope that he would be chosen. And he certainly had no intention of adding another wild "Gomer" tale to the long list already circulating the base by applying for the position.

On Tuesday morning, Terry and Jeff traversed the base to the police academy administration building, where hundreds of other Honor Guard hopefuls waited. After more than an hour, they reached the sign-up desk. Jeff bent down and placed his name on the roster where the clerk indicated. He and Terry started to move on, when the clerk, a pickle-faced airman first class, called Terry back.

"Airman, you didn't sign in."

"Oh, I'm not trying out. I'm just here for moral support, for my buddy." He tipped his head toward Jeff.

The clerk aimed the pen at Terry. "I'm sorry, but if you're here, you gotta sign the roster. That's the rule."

Knowing it would be futile to argue with a military rule, however unimportant it might be, Terry took a deep breath and signed his name to the roster.

They joined a line on the other side of the large assembly hall before Jeff nudged Terry with his elbow. "That's a kick— you trying out for the Honor Guard? Sorry, friend, but you must admit it is funny."

"Hey," Terry shrugged, "what can I say?" Even he could see the humor of the situation.

Their line inched forward. When Jeff reached the front, a sergeant measured his height and weight, then waved him on. The sergeant did the same with Terry. The men lined up as a group of officers strode back and forth in front of them, eyeing them carefully and scribbling notes on clipboards.

A sergeant called the men to attention, then stepped aside as a staff sergeant stepped forward and announced, "We were expecting 400 applicants today for the twelve Honor Guard positions. However, 850 of you showed up. Due to this large number, the evaluations will continue throughout tomorrow." He paused and scanned the airmen before him. "At this point, we are choosing individuals with a specific height and weight who possess a certain look. We have narrowed the number down to 400." The sergeant then announced that pictures would be taken of the remaining 400 applicants, while the rest would be excused. "We want to thank those of you who are not chosen for coming here today."

The long line of cadets inched toward the doorway, where a sergeant directed the chosen to the right, where a photographer waited to take their pictures, and the rejected applicants to the left and out of the building.

Jeff's shoulders drooped and his feet dragged as the two friends headed to their barracks. "I can't believe it! You made the cut, and I didn't, and I'm the one who wanted in so badly."

Terry didn't know what to say, since he, even more than his friend, was still stunned that he'd qualified with 399 other men for the first draft. "Hey, man, I'm really sorry."

"No big deal." Jeff slapped his friend on his shoulder and laughed good naturedly. "As soon as they see you march, they'll get rid of you too. So don't get too comfortable, Gomer."

Terry shook his head and grinned. What were the chances of being chosen for one of twelve positions from 400 of the United States Air Force's finest? "You're probably right."

"You know, I probably couldn't have gotten off for tomorrow's interview anyway since my flight is reviewing some pretty important material."

"Yeah, guess I'm lucky for flunking out of the flight, huh?" Terry smiled ruefully.

Jeff frowned and cocked his head to one side. "Hmm! Remember how you questioned why God would allow you to be put back in training?" A strange look of disbelief crossed Jeff's face. He waved his hand distractedly. "Naw."

"Naw," Terry echoed, spotting the line forming outside the mess hall. "Hey, it's suppertime. Let's get in line."

The news that Terry had survived the first cut had already reached many of his friends. "Hey, man, when they see you march, it's all over." He took their joshing in stride since he agreed they were probably right. The next morning, Terry headed to the administration building for the second phase of the recruitment process. Hour after boring hour passed as the Honor Guard officials continued their weeding process until

350 of the 400 had been dismissed. When the sergeant finished reading off the names and announced the next day's scheduled routine, Terry wondered whether the man had made a mistake. In a fog of doubt, he made his way back to the barracks.

The first person he met yelled across the compound, "Hey, Gomer, how'd you do? Did they see you march yet?"

Terry shook his head slowly. "Not yet."

The cadet ran over to Terry and squinted into his face. "What do you mean, not yet?"

"Well, I guess I'm still in the running."

The man's jaw dropped open. "You're kidding!"

The word spread throughout the flight. "Preacher boy made it through the second day of testing." The teasing continued throughout the evening. Even Sergeant Edding slapped his forehead in amazement that Terry had made it so far.

Terry's friends gathered about his bunk to rehash the news—Terry Johnson, Gomer Pyle himself, one of the fifty chosen out of 850—incredible.

Amid the laughter, a timid friend of Terry's ventured, "Maybe your God has a plan after all."

"Come on," one of the doubters added, "you gotta be kiddin'—Gomer? I mean you're a great guy, but Gomer?"

Terry shrugged for what seemed to be the hundredth time that evening. Even he had trouble stretching God's power to the President's Honor Guard's recruitment committee.

Later, alone in the darkness, stretched out on his bed, he couldn't shut off his mind. The President's Honor Guard? Washington, D.C.? The White House? Could such a thing really happen? He remembered seeing pictures on television of the White House during the Watergate hearings, of Arlington Cemetery and President Kennedy's grave, of the flag waving above the U.S. Capitol. To be there where it all happens! His imagination soared until reason grounded it. He punched his pillow and tried to get comfortable. His friends were right. It was a wild and crazy dream for the preacher boy who couldn't tell his left foot from his right.

The next morning, upon arrival at the assembly hall, Terry filled out a short questionnaire, then moved on to the interview, knowing no matter how well he did, it would all be for nothing once he had to demonstrate his marching ability. One good thing, he thought, I won't have to pull KP duty today.

"So, Airman Johnson," the interviewer inquired as he scanned Terry's application blank. "Where were you born?"

"Portland, Oregon, sir."

The recruiter continued his stream of questions. "How many children in your family? Where did you go to school? What are your hobbies?" Terry answered each one in turn.

The recruiter glanced down at his checklist. "Have you ever done any illegal drugs?"

Terry stopped. He thought back to his days in high school, when he and his friends played around with marijuana. He could lie. After all, who would know? He hadn't smoked the drug more than once or twice. Then he remembered his nickname, preacher boy. No, he thought, I've gotta do this God's way or not at all. Now's not the time to go it alone.

"Yes, sir—marijuana."

The recruiter snapped alert. He eyed the cadet suspiciously. "When and for how long?" His cold stare unnerved Terry.

Terry took a deep breath. "I used it once or twice in high school, sir—with my friends."

Pursing his lips into a disapproving bow, the recruiter nodded. "You know that this admission could destroy your chances of getting into the Honor Guard."

Terry straightened and took a ragged breath. "Yes, sir. I understand that, sir."

The recruiter leaned back in his chair and eyed him thoughtfully. "You could have lied."

"Yes, sir. I suppose I could have, sir." The recruiter studied Terry's face, then turned to the Honor Guard sergeant beside him. "Attach Airman Johnson's picture to his oral evaluation sheet and his written answer sheet." As an afterthought, he waved Terry off. "You're dismissed, Airman Johnson, until tomorrow at 0900 hours."

Terry walked out of the air-conditioned building into the late-afternoon sun and took a deep breath. "I guess I'm still in the running, at least until tomorrow, anyway."

Chapter Fourteen

Terry tormented himself that night more than any harassing his friends inflicted over his marching abilities. He, above all, knew his weaknesses. He'd spent years trying to live down the humiliation he'd suffered as a young child. When he finally climbed into bed and tried to sleep, he dreamed he was back at Irvington Elementary. He tossed about like a whirling dervish at the crackly voice of a laughing Mrs. Pennyworth. "You're a troublemaker. You're a retard, a dummy. You can't do it."

When reveille sounded, he wrestled to free himself from the bed linens twisted about his sweaty body. Even a warm shower couldn't relax him enough to feel confident about the upcoming review. Deciding not to try to eat a breakfast, Terry grabbed his Bible and went off to find a quiet spot where he could be alone. He finally made himself comfortable on the third stair of a deserted flight of steps behind the administration building.

He turned the pages of his Bible to the book of Psalms. His gaze rested on the words of Psalm 50:15. "Call upon me in the day of trouble; I will deliver you, and you will honor me" (NIV).

Terry stared down at the gravel beneath his feet for some time. "Thank You, Father, for reminding me that the honor and the glory belongs to You and You alone."

When he walked into the waiting area outside the large recreation room, the clerk handed him a card with the number

30 on it. Terry found a seat and sat down to await his turn. A few minutes later, a sergeant handed him a handwritten list of routines he would need to execute before the Honor Guard recruitment board.

"Enter room, salute, left face, right face, about face . . ." He read through the routine, command by command.

"Number thirty?" the clerk announced. Terry slowly got to his feet, straightening the wrinkles from his uniform as he gathered himself to his full height.

The sergeant took the paper and gestured toward the open door on the far side of the room. Terry could feel his heart pounding from his toes to his scalp as he strode across to where a female member of the Honor Guard waited. He paused at the door and smiled, looking for reassurance. In return, she gave him the traditional blind, impersonal stare as she announced him. "Airman Terry Johnson." The woman continued to stare straight ahead.

He took a deep breath and entered the large recreation room. A long table stretched out before him. Behind it sat a nine-person committee of stone-faced Honor Guard officers and other high-ranking air force sergeants. Terry's nerves tightened into a death knot as he stepped up to the table and looked at the waiting military brass. He'd never seen so many stripes in his entire life.

The goofy face of good old Gomer Pyle flashed through his mind. What am I doing here? His hands quivered, and his collar tightened into a vigilante noose. I don't belong here. Terrified more than he'd ever been, his mind froze. His body froze. Even his tongue seemed to numb with frostbite. He knew he was supposed to do something before sitting down, but what, he had no idea.

The people at the table glanced first at one another, then at him, then down at their clipboards. A captain who seemed to be in charge of the proceedings waved him toward the empty chair in front of the table. "Sit down, Airman Johnson, and tell us about yourself."

Blindly, he sat down as ordered. One by one the members of the panel asked him questions, scribbling down his answers as he spoke. After they ran the length of the table a second time, the captain who ordered him to be seated asked, "Is there anything you want to do or say?"

Terry stared straight ahead. "No, sir."

"Are you sure?"

Terry's gaze darted from one granite-chiseled face to the next. "No, sir, er, I mean, yes, sir."

The captain tapped his pencil on his clipboard and cleared his throat. "You're dismissed, airman."

As Terry stood to leave, he remembered the routine he was supposed to execute. Calm down, he told himself, as sweat trickled down the sides of his face. Calm down. Just get through the routine and get out of here as fast as you can. OK, now salute!

He snapped his left hand up to his forehead in a smart military salute and held it. A snicker rippled the length of the table. What are they laughing at? he wondered. He peered out of the corner of his eye at the hand touching his forehead. Oops! Wrong hand! Salute with the right hand, dummy!

He attempted to rectify his error with a right-handed salute. A few of the committee members snickered at his obvious state of confusion. To Terry, his entire military training seemed to have abandoned him. Oh, no, I must have been right the first time. He snapped off a second left-handed salute, then a second right-handed salute. The snickers grew to chuckles.

Slow down, buddy, he ordered himself. Get a grip. All he could do at this point was move on to the next requirement on the list. "Left face? Right face?" he mumbled to himself. "About face? Left face?"

Like a wind-up toy gone berserk, he turned right, then left, then about face, then left, then right, until he found himself turning in circles to a chorus of loud guffaws from the dignified air force brass. Each of the mortified cadet's frantic moves produced a fresh round of entertainment. The committee members abandoned all sense of military decorum. One officer doubled over, his forehead resting on his arm on the tabletop. His shoulders shook convulsively as he pounded his other fist on the table. The higher ranking officers wiped tears from their eyes as they struggled to retain their dignity in spite of their flushed faces. The officer at the end of the table appeared as if he might topple out of his chair onto the floor. One of the men, forsaking all pretense of self-control, stood up and leaned against the wall in an effort to catch his breath.

Horrified, Terry's eyes filled with humiliation when he realized they were laughing too hard by this time to even know what he was doing. "Excuse me for wasting your time," he mumbled. He saluted correctly again, turned, and strode toward the closed door. The female guard struggled to catch her breath enough to open the door. As she did, their eyes met. Embarrassed beyond reason, he frantically searched for something appropriate to say. "Do you think I have a chance?" he asked.

For a moment he thought she must not have heard his question over the panel's laughter, for she just stared in disbelief. Then, suddenly she shrieked and dropped to her knees. "That has to be the worst interview I've ever seen," she gasped between renewed bouts of hysteria. "You messed up completely—everything!"

The echo of laughter followed Terry from the room. All he could think of was to get away as fast as possible. He needed to talk with someone, someone who would understand. He glanced at his watch and rushed to the pay phones beside his barracks. He dropped in a handful of change and dialed his home phone number. The sound of his mother's silky, smooth voice more than 2,000 miles away brought tears to his eyes.

"Hi, Mom, this is Terry."

"Terry? Is something wrong, son?"

How does she always know? he wondered. "Oh, Mom, I really blew it this time. I was so nervous at the Honor Guard tryouts, I completely fell apart. I dropped my salute and just walked out."

She didn't speak immediately. "Oh, I'm so sorry. But who knows, maybe this is God's way of getting you released from the security police program."

"I don't know, Mom. I just don't know. Please pray for me."

"Tsk! You have to ask? I'll get some of the church members to pray with me too."

They talked for a few minutes longer, then said goodbye. Terry hung up the receiver and gazed out across the base. "This time I'm going to wait on You just like You said to do," he whispered. "I'm not going to question or doubt Your leading."

A growl in the pit of his stomach reminded him it was lunchtime. His friends were already eating when he got through line with his food.

Jeff waved from across the dining hall. "Hey, Johnson, over here."

Terry nodded and weaved between the tables until he arrived at the empty chair beside Jeff.

"So, how did it go this morning?" Jeff asked between mouthfuls of scalloped potatoes.

Terry groaned. "Don't ask."

"Why? What happened?"

Everyone at the table stopped eating long enough to hear Terry's reply.

Terry shook a forkful of lettuce in Jeff's face. "Hey, you're to blame, man. You're the one who got me into all of this, remember?"

"Into what? What happened at the interview?"

Terry told the whole embarrassing tale to his friends. The cadets choked with laughter. By now the event was funny to him as well.

Jeff wagged his fork in Terry's face. "You could have saved yourself the embarrassment and dropped out."

"What a fiasco." Terry stabbed at the white glob of gooey potatoes on his plate.

The next morning as he slipped into his first class, he was greeted with, "Hey, Mr. Honor Guard. When you leaving for D.C.?" For the entire week, as the applicants waited for the list of Honor Guard choices to be posted, instructors and cadets alike razzed Terry unmercifully.

"On the positive side," he quipped to Jeff after a cadet he'd never even met shouted, "Hey, Mr. Honor Guard," from across the road, "no one is calling me preacher boy or Gomer anymore. Now it's Mr. Honor Guard." Jeff laughed and shook his head.

On Thursday night, Sergeant Edding announced that the Honor Guard list would be posted in the morning and that only seven of the twelve positions had been filled.

Terry grimaced when the cadet sitting next to him whispered, "Hey, you gonna skip breakfast to check for your name?"

Throughout inspection on Friday morning, Terry seesawed between checking the list and ignoring it. What was the use, he finally decided. If someone saw him checking the list, a new wave of laughter would break out at his expense. He could just hear the story that would have developed by the time he returned to the barracks. Mr. Honor Guard actually had the audacity to look for his name on the list.

At lunch, one of the men from his unit slapped him on the shoulder. "Hey, congratulations, man, for making the Honor Guard."

A sick smile crossed Terry's face. "Right."

A few minutes later, a second cadet looked at him quizzically. "Don't you have an Honor Guard meeting right now?"

"Probably so." Terry picked up his tray and crossed to the serving line.

Behind him one of the members of his Bible-study group whispered, "So when do you leave for Washington?"

Terry pasted on a smile. "Any day now."

The afternoon passed without much more being said. After supper he headed for the PX. Toothpaste, deodorant, floss—thinking about the list of supplies he needed to replace, he didn't hear the entourage of vehicles coming up behind him until he heard a familiar voice. "That's him. That's Johnson."

Terry looked over his shoulder in time to see four black Lincoln Continentals slowing beside him. He could see Chris Pardon, one of the men Terry knew had made it to the Honor Guard, pointing at him from behind the tinted window. The lead vehicle stopped beside him, and the rear window silently lowered.

"Are you Airman Johnson?" the man closest to the open window asked.

Terry's mind raced, trying to remember what he might have done wrong this time. "Yes, sir."

The man inside the car scowled. "Do you know you are the first person in the history of the United States Air Force to hold up the President's Honor Guard? We've been waiting for you for two hours!"

"What? I-I-I beg your . . . excuse me, sir?" Terry stammered.

"Airman Johnson, you did apply for the Presidential Honor Guard, didn't you? You are one of the seven applicants selected. Didn't you check the list?"

Speechless, Terry shook his head, then stumbled into one of the cars as directed to be taken back to the training center. That evening, as the men gathered for their Friday-night Bible-study group, Terry waited for someone to mention the day's events. But since no one else from Terry's flight had made the third cut to fifty, only his closest friends and the six other men chosen knew that "Mr. Honor Guard" had indeed become Mr. Honor Guard. Since it wasn't something one mentioned with a "by the way," he kept quiet.

During the graduation ceremony, Terry felt only praise to God for helping him master the required skills that allowed him to finish thirteenth out of the seventy-five graduating cadets. The colonel of the police academy awarded the last of the air force security police badges, then smiled down at the graduating class. "I am pleased to announce that one of the seven airmen chosen for the President's Honor Guard is graduating from this class today."

Immediately the seventy-five police academy graduates craned their necks, trying to figure out which of the top cadets in the class had been good enough to be chosen.

"His name is Airman Terry Lyndon Johnson."

A stunned silence filled the room, followed by a series of gasps as the information registered. The nicknames "Mr. Honor Guard," "Gomer," and "preacher boy" buzzed through the audience, followed by a series of disbelieving No's. As if on cue, the audience broke into laughter, followed by raucous applause.

It was after graduation that Terry discovered he'd previously been assigned to Project Star Wars at the Patterson Air Force Base in Ohio. Now, his Honor Guard appointment superseded those orders.

"I can't believe it," one of his fellow cadets quipped. "Life isn't fair. You're going to a cushy job at the White House while I break out the long johns in North Dakota."

Jeff shook Terry's hand and looked him in the eyes. "You realize that if you hadn't been put back a week and forced to go casual, you wouldn't have been permitted to complete the Honor Guard tryouts."

Terry grinned and shrugged. "I tried to tell you that our God performs miracles."

"Humph! Where do I sign up?" a disgruntled cadet grunted.

Immediately after graduation, the flight broke up. The cadets headed out for their assigned missions. The members of the Friday-night Bible-study group assembled one last time.

Sergeant Edding pumped Terry's hand. "Boy, if I ever had doubts before about what God can do, they're erased now. Do you know that I was talking with a member of the panel about your evaluation sheets, and he said he doesn't remember writing anything down about you."

Jeff laughed and slugged Terry's shoulder. "It's like Daniel going before Nebuchadnezzar. Except this Daniel has two left feet."

SECTION THREE: HONOR-GUARD —— TRAINING
Bolling Air Force Base
Washington, D.C.
Autumn 1985

Chapter Fifteen

Travelers intent on making their flights to places known only to their travel agents and themselves rushed by as twenty-five air force men huddled together in the crowded waiting area of the air terminal. A mixture of humor and pathos permeated the tight little group as they said their last goodbyes. Knowing farewells were a constant part of military life didn't ease their pain.

"Now, we're going to keep in contact, right?" one of the men asked for the third or fourth time. "We can't risk losing the blessings we've gotten worshiping together these last few weeks, right?"

Terry reached into his canvas carry-on and pulled out a handful of religious tracts. "Here's a little reading material for each of you during the flight." The men laughed good-naturedly.

"It wouldn't be Terry if he didn't have some tract or book to hand out," one of the airmen joked.

"Hey, don't knock it," another interjected. "I'm going to appreciate having this by the time I land in North Dakota."

"North Dakota? Is that in the continental United States?" his buddy teased.

"Very funny!"

The airmen grew silent as the first boarding call that would separate the men was announced. "This is it, buddies." Terry lobbed his arms over the shoulders of the men on each side of him. "Remember if we never meet again on this earth, we have the promise of heaven. Let's pray together one more time." In the middle of Terry's prayer, they heard a second airman's boarding call announced over the public address system. By the end of their prayer, the men could no longer postpone the inevitable. As they pounded each other on the back and wished one another Godspeed, Terry wondered what the other passengers waiting for their flights might be thinking, seeing these tough-looking military men obviously choking back tears of farewell.

How can twenty-five strangers bond so completely in a few short weeks, Terry wondered, except through the grace of Jesus Christ? As the group broke up, there seemed nothing left to do but find an empty seat overlooking the airfield and read his last tract.

With his friends gone, his thoughts naturally turned toward his destination, Washington, D.C. Excitement sprang up unbidden at the thought of living for a time at the center of earthly power and politics. He'd never dreamed he'd actually get to visit, let alone work, in the capital city.

The southern drawl of the green-eyed, blond-haired ticket agent broke into Terry's reverie. "Trans World Airlines flight 2071 for Houston, St. Louis, and Washington, D.C., is now boarding. Those needing assistance or traveling with small children are asked to board at this time." Minutes later, the same agent announced the boarding of all passengers. Terry stuffed the tract into his jacket pocket, picked up his carry-on case, and joined the line forming at the entrance to the flight corridor.

Terry's heart pounded and his pulse raced when he first caught sight of the Washington Monument from the airplane window. He could hardly sit still as the jet banked over the city and he began identifying famous landmarks. The Capitol dome, the White House, the Jefferson Memorial, the Tidal Basin, and the Pentagon each held his attention as the plane descended for a landing at Washington National Airport. He gnawed on his lower lip in anticipation when the plane taxied into the terminal.

Terry waited as his fellow passengers shoved, bullied, and clawed their way to the front of the plane to disembark. Finally he got up, removed his carry-on case from the overhead compartment, and walked forward to the exit. The excitement he felt must have shown on his face, for the female flight attendant at the door asked, "Is this your first flight to D.C.?"

He battled the grin that threatened to overpower his nonchalant façade. "Yes, ma'am."

"I thought so," she confided. "I still remember my first visit to D.C."

Inside the terminal, he paused to absorb the scene—a sea of gray suits, ranging from light to charcoal, all sporting neckties of red and maroon and all rushing about like a colony of ants under attack by an eight-year-old commando. He allowed himself to be drawn along with the crowd to the luggage area, where he jostled with tourists, skycaps, uniformed chauffeurs, lower-level politicians, and bureaucrats for luggage. Curbside, the frantic mass of humanity battled for taxis. He looked at the frenzy and decided he wasn't in much of a rush after all. I'll wait. I have all day, he thought. He waited until the first surge of humanity passed, then signaled for a cab.

Handing the driver the letter he'd been given before leaving Texas, Terry asked him to take the scenic route to Bolling Air Force Base. Terry leaned forward and peered out the side window as the driver maneuvered the vehicle through the tangle of one-way and blocked streets in the capital city. Everywhere he gazed he saw scenes lifted from his high-school history book.

"Look! Look! There's the White House." Terry stared at 1600 Pennsylvania Avenue until it disappeared from sight. "Imagine. Just imagine."

The driver grinned back at the eager young man. "First time in D.C.?"

"Oh, yeah, can you tell?"

The cabbie snorted, then fell victim to Terry's contagious enthusiasm. "That's the FBI building over there." As the meter clicked off the charges, the driver pointed out the other side of the car. "See the building that looks like a castle? It and the surrounding buildings are the Smithsonian Institute. My wife drags me there on a regular basis to see the First Ladies' inauguration gowns, as if they're going to change from year to year. I prefer the antique airplanes myself."

Terry wet his lips in anticipation. "I'm going to have to get back here as soon as possible."

When he pumped the cabdriver for Washington trivia, the driver was only too willing to act as guide and entertainer. The cabbie slowed as they passed the Washington Monument.

"This is neat, man. This is neat!" Terry repeated again and again. When the Jefferson Memorial came into view, Terry's breath caught in his throat, and his eyes filled with tears. He craned his neck around to catch one last glimpse as the driver headed toward the bridge that spans the Potomac River.

The driver eyed Terry through the rearview mirror. "And now, a few minutes on the freeway, and we'll be at your new home, Bolling Air Force Base."

At the gates to the base, Terry showed the guards his letter and was waved through. The taxi stopped in front of a building marked United States Air Force Honor Guard. Terry grabbed his luggage and paid the driver. "Thanks for the tour."

The cabbie grabbed his hand. "Thank you for sharing your first view of D.C. with me. It was like, what is the line in that TV ad—seeing it again for the first time." The driver waved and drove off.

Terry watched the taxicab disappear, then turned to survey his new home. Suddenly Steve, one of the seven men chosen at the police academy in San Antonio, bounded out of the building. He ran to Terry and engulfed him in a bearhug as if they were long-lost buddies, though they only knew each other by sight. "I got here earlier. You're only the second to arrive, Johnson. Hey, let me show you around." He grabbed Terry's duffle bag and led him into the building. "We won't actually meet our T.I. until tomorrow."

Bewildered, Terry listened as Steve pointed out the showers, the lounge, and the laundry room, then the room Terry had been assigned. "Let me help you unpack."

By the time Steve settled him into his new quarters, another airman arrived, and Steve abandoned Terry to start his next tour. Terry sat on the edge of the bed and stared at the barren room. A moment of uncertainty caused him to place his head in his hands. Self-doubts flooded through his brain. He already knew that the Honor Guard training was one of the toughest in the air force. One person in six washes out before the end of his training. Yet on the good side, the Honor Guard personnel he'd met at Lackland assured him that as long as he wanted to be there and to try, he would eventually pass. He could only fail by giving up.

He'd laughed to himself when the sergeant told him that. He doesn't know me, Terry thought. If I've learned anything during my lifetime, I've learned never to give up. The man had said that Terry would determine how fast he would get through the Honor Guard training program.

"You set your own limit," the sergeant had explained. "It's according to how fast you learn your equipment. Some people finish in three weeks. Others take eight or ten weeks to pass the examinations."

Terry remembered the exams at the police academy. He'd worked hard to qualify in each of the required areas and finally succeeded. He straightened, stood up, and removed his jacket. If I did it there, he reasoned, I can do it here.

He looked forward to learning how to spin the rifles in the air, how to form a cordon for visiting dignitaries, how to perform each of the flashy maneuvers he'd heard so much about. He never dreamed that his first lesson would be cutting the buttons off his uniform jacket.

"We cut them off, then pin them in place in order to keep the eagle perfectly straight," the unit's training instructor explained.

He learned to arrange the buttons by size in his locker. He learned to starch and iron the sleeves of his blue uniform paper thin only to have the inspection team crumple them up and order him to start all over. His regulation wardrobe consisted of three pair of pants, three formal jackets, three long-sleeved air force shirts, as well as an overcoat. If he thought he'd learned how to set up his locker in basic training, Terry discovered the Honor Guard has its own idea of the perfect locker, a process that takes three hours to set up every morning. If, during morning inspection, the sergeant finds a piece of lint in someone's locker, he will crumble the contents of the locker and order the hapless guard to set it up all over again in an hour's time, or the entire bay will suffer. This is done to promote teamwork, since one man could never complete the task in an hour's time. In one week's time, the guard trainees of a bay become like brothers and function as a smooth, well-run team. This teamwork then carries over into the other areas of training, with the guards each helping one another to improve their skills.

Since the Honor Guard requires that a guard's uniform be without wrinkle or bulge, the guard will cut the lining out of the overcoat to make it hang smoothly. In order to keep their neck scarves wrinkle-free, they pin a strip of cardboard to the scarf and fasten it around their necks, creating a cardboard neck brace. The triple-sole patent leather shoes with their metal taps on the toes and the horseshoe-shaped taps on the heels weigh three pounds apiece and have a three-inch-high heel. Due to the hours of marching and standing at attention, a guard will wear out a pair of shoes every six months.

The Honor Guard trainees live in a dormitory instead of in barracks. Two trainees share each room except for the bay leader, who rooms alone. Terry soon learned an unwritten code in the Honor Guard was to sleep under the bed instead of on it in order to keep the starched and pressed sheets fresh and wrinkle-free for the entire week.

Terry continued having trouble not only remembering which was his right and which was his left foot, but he also had trouble keeping his mouth closed while in formation. Since tourists found it humorous to ask the guardsmen questions, trying to make a guard talk on duty, Terry's naturally sanguine personality and his desire to please proved to be a constant problem for him.

Chapter Sixteen

The T-flight instructor ordered the Honor Guard trainees to attention. "This morning I am going to teach you men a valuable lesson—not to talk while in formation."

For the most part, guard training proved to be more laid-back than basic training had been. Yet, the instructors demanded nothing less than perfection from the men. "You will represent the United States Air Force at the Tomb of the Unknown Solider, at the White House, at the National Archives, at the Pentagon, at formal banquets, and at funerals in Arlington Cemetery. Grannys, teenagers, as well as little kids, will try to make you laugh. Teenaged girls will try to pick up on you. They'll stuff notes and phone numbers in your pockets." He eyed the trainees for emotional reactions. No one so much as blinked. "If the harassment becomes physical, you must stay at attention until a security guard comes to your rescue.

"You will be forced to stand at attention for hours during long and boring speeches. Should you flake, the press will record it for posterity, yours and the United States Air Force's. And I don't need to tell you what that means."

For a guard to "flake," or pass out while in formation, or in flight, as it was called, brought ridicule and shame on the guard personally and on his branch of service. All the trainees keenly felt the competition between the five branches of service represented in the Honor Guard—the army, navy, marines, air force, and the coast guard. In addition, the guard would be cited, and two citations terminated his service.

"Now regarding talking while in flight, it is never, ever done. Johnson, do you understand?"

"Yes, sir!" Terry snapped, staring straight ahead.

"Airman Johnson, you just did exactly what I told you not to do. You just talked while in flight. Now, I'm going to work with you to break you of this habit, do you understand?"

"Yes, sir!" The words were out before Terry realized what he was doing.

"See? You're doing it again. I want you to run as fast as you can down to the corner. I want to hear you tell the Stop sign four times that you will not talk while in flight again."

Terry didn't see the laugh marks teasing the corners of the T-flight instructor's mouth.

"Now run!"

Terry ran the half-mile down the road to the sign as instructed. This is silly, he thought, talking to a Stop sign. When he reached the corner, he skidded to a stop in front of the sign and snapped to attention. "I will not talk in flight again." His words came out in short, painful gasps.

"I will not talk in flight again." He repeated the vow two more times, then raced back to the waiting instructor. When Terry had resumed his place in the lineup, the instructor strode over to him.

"Now, Johnson, what have you learned today?"

"Not to—" he cut himself off midsentence. His eyes widened in horror.

"Johnson," the T-flight instructor chuckled to himself, "you and your pledge to the Stop sign will go down in Honor Guard history."

Terry soon learned that history does repeat itself. His reputation as a Christian followed him. He became the bay's chaplain guide by default. Anyone with a personal problem or a problem at home sought him out for counsel. By the second week of training, four of the seven men in his bay met with him after hours to talk and study the Bible.

The training flight shared the same dormitory with the regular members of the Honor Guard, but that was all. The air force allowed no communication between the trainees and the official guardsmen. Each floor had a fully equipped laundry, which everyone shared. But should a guard enter while a trainee was washing his clothes, the trainee was not to speak.

One afternoon, Terry heaved his laundry bag over his shoulder and picked up his Bible, then went to wash his clothes. All during the first week he'd been praying that God would show him a way to get to church. Free from 4:30 on Friday afternoon until 7:00 a.m. on Monday, he had the time but not the transportation to attend church services in neighboring Georgetown, as there were no organized services on base. So far his prayer hadn't been answered.

Terry walked into the empty laundry room and stuffed his first load of dirty clothes into a washing machine. He settled himself down on one of the shiny plastic-and-chrome chairs against the wall and opened his Bible. "Now," he muttered to himself, "where did I leave off this morning?"

Intent on his search, Terry failed to hear a second individual enter the laundry room until the intruder shut the door behind him. Terry looked up and smiled at the tall black guardsman crossing the room to the empty washing machine next to his. He also noted the sergeant's stripes on the man's sleeve. The guard smiled back, then glanced down at the book in Terry's lap.

"You're a Christian, huh? Me too." The man dumped his laundry onto the floor and sorted the light clothes from the darks. After he stuffed his first load into the washer and started the machine, he turned to Terry. "Reginald Washington. My friends call me Reggie."

Terry stood and introduced himself. The two men talked about religion, about military life, and life in general while the machines processed their clothing. When Terry's washing machine stopped, he put the clean clothes into a dryer, then started his second load of wash.

They continued their conversation between loading and unloading machines. Terry removed his last load of wash from the dryer and started folding it, when Reggie switched the subject from home and childhood back to religion.

"What church do you attend, Terry?"

"I'm a Seventh-day Adventist."

Reggie shook his head. "Oh, it must be pretty difficult for you to get to church around here."

"Yes, I've been praying about it all week, and I don't have any answers yet." Terry shook one of his bottom sheets in the air, hoping to locate a missing sock.

"I don't know where you'd find a Seventh-day Adventist church around here, but how would you feel about going to church on Sunday with me and my buddy, Coop?" Reggie watched Terry's face for reactions as he spoke. "You could have your Saturday worship alone on base, then your Christian fellowship at a small church a number of air force personnel formed just off the base."

Terry stacked his clean laundry on top of his laundry bag. "But I'm just a trainee. You and I aren't even suppose to . . ."

"Yeah, I didn't think of that. If another member of the Honor Guard saw us leave base together, we'd both be in trouble."

Terry picked up his laundry and headed toward the closed door.

"Here, let me get that for you." Reggie leaped for the door, but before opening it he cautioned, "Hey, don't say anything to anyone about our, uh, talk."

"You got it." Terry stepped into the hallway. The laundry room door closed behind him.

He hurried to his locker and put away his clothes. The rest of the week passed, and he forgot about his laundry room encounter. On Friday night the dormitory emptied out for the weekend. After a hard week on duty, most guardsmen headed into Georgetown for what they called "R 'n R," which translated meant hard drinking and womanizing.

Terry settled down to sleep early that Friday night. The next morning, after breakfast, he grabbed his Bible, writing paper, and a stack of Christian magazines and walked down by a small stream on base. There he found a quiet spot where he could spend a few of the Sabbath hours alone. An Indian summer breeze ruffled the pages of his Bible as he read and then prayed.

Taking a pad of writing paper, Terry penned a letter home. ". . . Right now, I picture you sitting in church singing 'Family of God' and trying to imagine what I might be doing . . ." When he finished the letter, he read a copy of *Message* magazine through from cover to cover, then followed with an old copy of *Insight*. As he read the college advertisement on the back cover, he sighed. I never get homesick during the week, but come Sabbath . . .

The day passed slowly. He slept for a while in the sunlight, then read an issue of *Guide*. The sun disappeared behind the Virginian hills as he made his way back to the silent dormitory. Opening the door to his room, he spotted an envelope with his name on it on the floor. He picked it up and opened it.

"For church tomorrow, be at the west side of the dormitory near the pine trees by 8:15 a.m. When a car stops, hop in."

Chapter Seventeen

Terry balanced first on one foot, then the other, blowing warm breath on his hands. He could smell a touch of winter in the crisp morning air. An unseasonably cool autumn breeze whispered through the branches of a cluster of young evergreens. The trees supplied him with a perfect blind for anyone coming out of the Honor Guard dormitory. Except for one or two early risers heading for the mess hall, most men still on base were sleeping off their Saturday-night adventures.

He turned his collar up and burrowed deeper into the woolen confines of his jacket. He'd just about given up hope when a gray Pontiac LE whipped around the corner of the dormitory and screeched to a stop in front of the trees. The back door flew open. Praying that he wasn't hopping into some four-star general's car by accident, Terry bounded out from behind the trees and jumped into the automobile. Before he could close the door, the vehicle leaped forward.

Driving straight down the center of the highway, Reggie turned and grinned at Terry. "Mornin', little bro. Meet Sergeant Wayne Cooper, Coop for short, on Sunday mornin', at least." Terry had heard about the black sergeant with the round, friendly grin. Coop reached back and shook Terry's hand. "So you're from Portland, Oregon?"

Terry grinned. "Yes, sir."

Coop shook his head. "No *sirs* on Sunday morning, OK?"

"OK, sir, er, I mean, right." Terry leaned back against the seat and tried to relax. Reggie eyed Terry through the rearview mirror. "That's right. On Sunday we're strictly brothers in Christ."

Terry's eyes shone with relief. "That sounds good to me."

Reggie drove with his arm on the back of the seat. "So what part of Portland are you from? I visited Oregon once."

"I grew up in northeast Portland, but my folks live in Troutdale now. That's a one-horse town about ten miles east of the city."

Reggie laughed. "All I remember about Portland is the bridges. I've never seen so many bridges clustered over one small river in my life."

Terry nodded. "And they're always building more."

"Let me tell you a little about our church, Terry," Coop interjected. "We call it the True Light Community Church. It's a nondenominational church, started and operated mainly by air force personnel. We have about 150 members."

"That is neat. I am really impressed. I'd love to raise up a church someday," Terry admitted.

The three men conversed like old friends during the short ride to the church. Once they entered the small sanctuary, the congregation welcomed Terry into their midst immediately. Terry felt at home with the enthusiastic singing and the alive, Spirit-led worship service. As he looked around, he saw a group of sincere Christians worshiping their Saviour. He knew that, if Reggie and Coop asked, he'd be coming back.

After the service, when they dropped him off by the dormitory, Terry checked each direction to be certain no one would see him get out of the car. "I feel so silly, like I'm playing 'spy.'"

Reggie reminded him that the clandestine meetings would need to continue only for a few weeks. Once he qualified and became a full-fledged guardsman, there would be no problem.

By the end of the third week, the first of the seven new recruits completed the training program and joined the Honor Guard. One by one the rest of the trainees qualified during the next five weeks. At the eight-week point, Terry tried out. As he completed the last of the examinations, he felt good about his performance. Confident, he waited for the results.

"Johnson, you did just fine on everything," his T-flight instructor told him. "However, the committee feels you're not quite ready yet. We are going to keep you in T-flight for a while longer."

Terry's heart and spirits crumbled. Finally he'd done something right in the military but was still being held back. Since the Honor Guard is a voluntary appointment, he knew he could leave at any time. He wondered if this was the time. He wrestled with two voices. One said, "Hang on," and the other said, "Forget it. Pack it in. Did you really think you, of all people, could make it into the guard?"

Being all alone in the trainee's section of the dormitory didn't help his morale. Since Terry no longer had a Bible-study group in the evening, he decided to take a long walk after supper. When Terry returned to his room, he sat down at his desk to write a few letters. Words failed him as he tried to explain his failure to his mother. How could she understand that this failure was different from all the others he'd endured? Yet it was. He banged his fist on the desktop. It truly was. He'd just given up on writing the letter when he heard a tap on his door. News of Terry's failure to qualify had reached Reggie and Coop. The door flew open and Reggie stepped in, slamming the door immediately behind himself.

Terry leaped to his feet. "What are you doing here? If you get caught you're gonna be in—"

Reggie gestured for Terry to stop talking. "I know, I know. I can't stay. So grab your laundry bag and meet me in the laundry room in five minutes—that's an order!" Without a backward glance, Reggie stepped out into the hall.

Still feeling the sting of rejection, Terry didn't really want to be around anyone. He'd as much as made up his mind about leaving the guard training program. "I might as well get this over with," he mumbled to himself. "I can't hibernate in this room forever. Besides, if I don't meet Reggie, he'll probably do something dumb like come back in here."

Like a man prodded toward his execution, Terry made his way to the laundry room. As he stepped inside, the door slammed shut behind him. "So, I'm here. Now what?"

Reggie sat atop one of the folding tables. "Hey, where's that Johnson spirit everyone always talks about?"

Coop stepped in behind Terry and closed the laundry room door more quietly. "Come on, man, we know you're discouraged, but you can't quit now!"

Feeling like a petulant child, Terry pursed his lips. "Who said anything about quitting?"

Coop dropped into one of the plastic-and-chrome chairs along the wall. "The word is out, Johnson. But, you know you can't do it, man."

Reggie took up where Coop left off. "God has a purpose for you in the guard. Look how He's led you so far. There's been a reason for every stumbling block you've experienced since you joined the military—right? And I know there is a good one this time too."

Terry leaned against the doorjamb. His head drooped almost to his chest.

"Come on, Johnson, get your head on straight," Reggie demanded.

Coop leaned back and crossed his arms on his chest. "Don't lose faith now, not when you're so close to reaching your goal."

"All my friends are in the guard now. I'm all alone."

Coop let out an exasperated sigh. "Do you believe that? You're sounding like a spoiled eight-year-old."

Impatient, Reggie leaped off the table. "We're here to pray with you, to help you regain your faith in God's leading."

Afraid to kneel together lest someone burst in on them, the three men formed a huddle. As Terry's friends pleaded with God to strengthen his faith, a calm assurance filled Terry. He knew before the prayer ended that he would stay with the training program until God directed him to do otherwise.

On Monday morning, the new training flight arrived, and instead of being made bay leader, thus having a room of his own, Terry was issued a roommate—Frank Jones. From the moment Frank walked into the room, a wave of cool antagonism came with him.

"Good to have you here, man." Terry introduced himself

and reached to shake Frank's hand. The other man reluctantly complied. Terry continued as if he'd received a kiss from his mother. "As you can see, I'm already set up on this side of the room. So where do you call home?"

"Garden Grove, California." Frank turned his back on Terry and started unpacking his belongings.

"Oh, really? I'm from Oregon—Portland."

Frank continued unpacking as if he were alone in the room. Terry watched Frank bring out a silver framed picture and place it on his night stand.

From his own side of the room, Terry glanced at the face of the laughing blond-haired woman, her blond hair backlit by the afternoon sunlight. "Girlfriend?"

Frank straightened abruptly. "Wife!"

Terry blinked in surprise at the man's vehemence. "Lovely woman.

"Fine," Terry mumbled to himself, "have it your way, at least for now." While Frank set up his locker, Terry sat down at his desk for his personal worship. He dropped a Carl Parker cassette into his tape deck and opened his Bible. The singer's rich baritone voiced filled the room with "My Soul Is Anchored in the Lord." Terry glanced over his shoulder in time to see a look of disgust cross Frank's face.

Measuring each movement with studied deliberation, Frank took a cassette from his desk drawer and dropped it into his recorder. The powerful strains of the Mormon Tabernacle Choir singing "Come, Come Ye Saints" overpowered the soloist. Satisfied with the volume, Frank sat down at this desk and opened the *Book of Mormon.*

Terry reached over and turned off his tape deck. Oh, no, he thought, not another Rick. It had been one thing to live in a barracks of fifty men with someone who detested him, but living in the same room with Frank's barely concealed hostility? He stared down at his open Bible.

"What do I do, Lord? I don't believe it! What is this guy's problem?" Then Terry recalled the amazing things God had done for and through him. "OK, Father, I know You can handle my disagreeable roommate."

Chapter Eighteen

Terry rolled his eyes skyward when Frank returned from his first day of guard training and mumbled something about going to call his wife. "Don't you think you'd better set up your—" The door slammed behind Frank before Terry could add the word *locker*.

This guy has a terrible attitude problem. How can I witness to him, Terry wondered, if I can't get him to acknowledge my presence in the room? He knew talking wouldn't work, since Frank never stayed in his presence long enough to listen. And giving him tracts was equally as hopeless. Then he remembered Elder Matula. He remembered how the Bible teacher didn't preach or condemn. Instead, he transformed Terry through kindness.

One thing Terry did know about Frank. The man was desperately homesick for his wife, Laura. He also knew that if Frank didn't get busy preparing his locker soon, he'd be up all night doing it. So while Frank was on the telephone, Terry set up both his and Frank's lockers. He wondered what Frank would say when he returned to the room and discovered the tedious task completed. Rather than hang around to find out, Terry went to get acquainted with their next-door neighbors, Ken and Sandy.

A few minutes later, Frank passed by the open door of the room where Terry and a group of cadets were talking.

"Hey, come join us," Terry called.

With hardly a glance in Terry's direction, Frank kept on walking.

"He's really not a bad guy once you get to know him," Sandy quipped.

Ken agreed. "Yeah, I was talking with him just this morning. Seemed nice enough then."

"I guess." Terry got to his feet and headed for the door. "Well, he sure doesn't like me."

Ken looked at his roommate, Sandy, then back at Terry. "Oh, you've got to understand. Frank says he's not used to, uh, being around, uh, black people. It's not that he's prejudiced. He's just not used to . . ."

Terry raised his hands defensively. "Hey, it's OK. I learned long ago that it's only a problem when I let it become a problem. Look, I gotta get some sleep; I'm beat."

By the time Terry entered his room, the lights were off, and Frank was in bed. Oh, well, Terry thought as he slipped out of his fatigues and into his pajamas, one day down, and who knows how many more to go?

During the days that followed, Terry inundated Frank with kindness. If Frank left the room with his bed unmade, Terry made his bed. When he did his own laundry, Terry volunteered to do Frank's laundry as well. Terry ironed Frank's sheets and starched and ironed his shirts. He kept the room spotless, doing his share of the work and Frank's without ever mentioning it to anyone.

Occasionally Frank walked into the room while Terry and his friends were discussing the Bible or when Terry was counseling someone who'd come for advice about a personal problem. Frank always managed to escape as quickly as possible, as if being in the room might contaminate his own religious faith.

No matter how hard he fought it, Frank began to change. At first he barely acknowledged Terry's kindness; then Frank responded with mumbled "thank-yous." After a few weeks, Frank hung around when the men gathered for their Bible study—not participating or even indicating that he was listening, but within easy hearing distance.

One night, Terry stood at the sink in the washroom, brushing his teeth when Frank entered. Terry grinned and mouthed a garbled Hi, then went on with his brushing. Frank laid his toothbrush and toothpaste tube on the sink beside Terry. He stared into the wall-length mirror at Terry's reflection for several seconds before speaking. "All right, what gives?"

"What do you mean?" Bubbles sputtered from Terry's mouth.

Frank shook his head vigorously. "I don't understand why you are being so nice to me, when I've been so rotten to you. Why are you doing all these things for me?"

Terry bent down and rinsed out his mouth with water, then stood back up. "I didn't do it for you; I did it for my Lord."

"Well, I'm impressed." Frank stared down at the floor for a moment. "I don't know too many people who live their religion. I've been watching you—and listening."

"You have?"

"You'll be qualifying for the guards soon and moving out. I'd like to hear more about your Jesus before you leave."

Terry couldn't believe what he was hearing. But he certainly wouldn't pass up such a ripe opportunity. "I've known about Jesus my entire life. When I was a baby my mother used to take me to church, and I'd scream throughout the entire service. Then when I had trouble in elementary school, my mother transferred me to a Christian school." He nibbled on his lower lip before continuing. "But I have to admit, while I knew about Jesus all those years, I didn't really know Him for myself. Then, at the end of my senior year, I picked up a tract off the concrete in downtown Portland, and that tract made the difference in my life."

Eagerly, he told Frank about the tract. "The man's name was Reverend Wonderful. When the man died, Christ couldn't find his name on the books of heaven. To make a long story short, Reverend Wonderful had been so caught up in the religious scene that he forgot to get acquainted with Jesus, to accept the incredible sacrifice of the Saviour's death.

"I thought about the story of Reverend Wonderful and knew I had to change. I had to stop playing at religion and become a practicing, living Christian." Terry whispered a silent prayer for help, then continued. "Frank, Jesus Christ died for you too.

He loves you and longs to have you love Him in return."

Then Terry told about how God led him through each crisis since joining the military, opening seemingly impossible doors to bring him to the Honor Guard. "There's nothing like it. Even at the times my faith was at its weakest, Jesus has been right beside me, working out His plan for my life. And He'll continue to, long after I leave the guard."

Frank stared down at the sink. "And this is why you've been so nice to me these last few weeks, in spite of my, uh, attitude?"

"That's right. Jesus commanded me to be nice to you. He said, 'Love one another as I have loved you.' The old Terry would have popped you in the nose a time or two." Terry laughed at the surprise on Frank's face.

Frank studied Terry for a few seconds. Then haltingly, like a toddler taking his first steps, he said, "I think it's time for me to accept your Jesus into my heart."

"I-I-I—" Terry's toothbrush clattered into the sink. He'd never expected Frank to come so far so fast.

"So, what do I have to do?" Frank grinned a lopsided smile.

"Uh, pray, ask forgiveness for your sins, and then invite Jesus into your heart."

"Let's do it."

"Here?"

Frank shrugged. "Why not?"

"You're right. Why not?" The two knelt down by the row of sinks and prayed together. They returned to their room and talked late into the night. Frank had myriads of questions that kept Terry scrambling to his Bible for answers. The first rays of dawn angled through the venetian blinds on their bedroom window before they agreed to save a few things to talk about the next evening.

They talked with one another at every opportunity. They were walking back to the dormitory after supper one night when Frank stopped and turned toward Terry. "I've been telling my wife all about you—and about my decision for Christ. I love her so much. I want her to be with me on this."

"That's not something one person can decide for another,

Frank. Give her time," Terry warned. "Remember it took you awhile."

"You're right." Frank started walking again. "She's flying in for a visit this weekend. Maybe you can stick around and talk with her?"

"Sure thing."

"You're going to be qualifying in the next few days. It won't be the same once we're in the guard. I'm going to miss our talks." Frank kicked at a pebble on the walkway. "Do you realize that I would never have found you as a friend and found Christ as my Saviour if you hadn't been kept back from qualifying these extra weeks?"

"You're probably right," Terry admitted, "though we would have been in the Honor Guard together."

Frank gave a wry smile and shook his head. "Terry, you know how I felt about blacks when I entered the training program. Out of 150 guardsmen, I never would have taken the time to get to know you if we hadn't been roommates. I don't know which will shock my wife more, discovering my experience with Christ is real or discovering that the best friend I've been writing about is black."

Chapter Nineteen

"Johnson, do you know you have set a record here in the Honor Guard training program?" The T-flight instructor strutted back and forth in front of where Terry stood at attention. "That's right, a record—twelve weeks. We've never had a trainee hang around so long. You must have liked us too much to leave." The instructor chuckled at his own humor, as did the three other T-flight examiners. "So I suppose now you think it's time to retake your final examinations?"

Terry swallowed the temptation to respond to the man's question, staring straight ahead at the horizon. You're not going to catch me talking while in flight this time, he mused.

The officers put Terry through the first three areas of evaluation—leaving the marching until last. Left, right, backward, forward, up and down in front of the committee he marched, executing the examiner's commands with a precision worthy of any military personnel, including a prestigious honor guardsman. The drill sergeant called him to a halt, then strode over to where the three other examiners waited.

His adrenalin level pumping to incredible heights, Terry waited for the results of his performance. He knew he'd done well. I did better than well, he admitted to himself. I can't think of any area in which I might have even hesitated!

The drill sergeant returned. A frown of displeasure filled his face. "Come on and march with me around the building, Airman Johnson." Once they were out of hearing distance of the other men, the sergeant shouted a stream of questions at

Terry. "Why didn't you listen to me? I can't understand how you could have messed up so badly after training for such a long time. What is wrong with you, anyway?"

Terry gulped back tears of disappointment but remained silent. He had no answers to the instructor's questions. The sergeant called Terry to a halt beside the administration building. "All right, let's go through the commands one more time and see if you can get them right this time. Left face. Right face. About face."

The sergeant left him facing the brick building. Terry knew he'd executed the commands with clipped precision. A minute passed, two minutes, without the sergeant's saying a word. Finally the sergeant ordered him to do an about face. Terry snapped about, only to come face to face with a bucket of ice cold water. He sputtered while trying to stand at attention until ordered to do otherwise. The four examiners laughed.

"Welcome to the Honor Guard, Airman Johnson." The commander pounded Terry on the back. "The pail of water is your baptism into the President's Honor Guard, a serious guard tradition, I might add. You are now officially in flight, a JEEP—Junior Enlisted Experimental Personnel. You will begin your service Monday morning at Arlington National Cemetery. At ease, man, at ease!"

Terry cracked an uncertain smile. "You're serious?"

The examiners laughed and pounded him on the back. "You got it."

He'd worked hard, harder than he'd ever worked before in his life, to learn the Honor Guard way to walk, the Honor Guard way to talk, and the Honor Guard way to look. He'd learned to shoot as well as toss rifles. He'd practiced the 100-steps-per-minute cadence of the Honor Guard march. And now, he'd made it! Terry's face beamed with delight.

He was assigned to his friend Sergeant Washington's unit in the second element of the Honor Guard. The United States Air Force Honor Guard, established in 1948, functions as an elite ceremonial unit but has four divisions of duties, or elements: the first element is the flag bearers; the second element is the pallbearers at Arlington National Cemetery; the third, the firing party for twenty-one gun salutes; and the fourth element is the twenty-five-member M-1 rifle drill team. All elements serve at ceremonial banquets, White House dinners, and official functions for foreign dignitaries. The Honor Guard fulfills everything around the President that requires military representation.

The next few weeks of training kept Terry busy and exhausted at the end of the day. And I used to go out of my way to lift weights, he thought as he and his teammates lifted a mock casket, loaded with sandbags, onto their shoulders and carried it the required distance. At Arlington National Cemetery, they went step by step through the traditional military funeral. He remembered films he'd seen in high-school history class of President Kennedy's funeral. He realized that, sooner or later, he'd be required to perform the routine.

His friend and immediate superior, Sergeant Washington, admitted that by far, Terry was the most difficult JEEP he'd ever had to train. Then in the next breath, he added, ". . . and the best friend I've made of all of them."

At the same time, the air force was processing the paperwork to secure presidential clearance for the newest guardsman. Military security did a complete background check on Terry, questioning neighbors and friends in Oregon. A member of his fourth-grade class, then in college, was asked to tell everything she ever knew about him. People who hadn't seen him in years were questioned about his honesty.

Terry settled into the new routine at Bolling, going out of his way to make friends with the men in his element, especially his new roommate, Carl, a blue-eyed, blond guard from Mississippi. They quickly established a comfortable rapport. It was a tradition on weekends for the squadron to party on Friday night at the 21st Century, a place in Georgetown.

Terry spent his first Friday night in the Honor Guard alone in the dormitory studying his Bible. The next Friday, as Carl changed clothes for an evening of partying, he invited Terry to go with him. "It's a victory party for all you new guys coming into the guard. There's free beer and the works." Terry could hear a note of hopefulness in his friend's southern drawl.

"Thanks, but I think I'll stay here in the dorm."

Carl peered at Terry strangely. "What are you going to do tonight, then?"

Terry cleared his throat. "Thought I'd spend some time reading my Bible."

"I've seen you doing that all week long. Just what do you know about the Bible, anyway?"

Terry laughed. "Not enough—that's for sure. That's why I'm reading more."

"Hmm!" Carl thought for a moment, then walked to the door. "I need to talk to you sometime about that."

The next Friday night, while the other guardsmen prepared to leave for Georgetown, Carl puttered about the room.

One of the guardsmen burst into the room. "Hurry up, Carl. You're going to keep everyone waiting."

Carl glanced over at Terry, to where he sat writing a letter home. "I'm staying here for the Bible study."

Always careful never to "talk" religion unless someone asked, Terry snapped alert at his roommate's announcement. They spent the evening sharing the religious experiences of their childhoods. As they each went to sleep for the night, Carl called to Terry, "Let's do this again next week."

The next Friday night Carl invited a few of his friends to join them. When members of Terry's prayer group from training learned he'd started up his meetings again, they came also.

Four guardsmen passed the open door on their way to town. "Hey, you going with us, Carl?" one of the men called.

Carl laughed and waved. "Thanks anyway. I think I'll save a few bucks this week."

As the other three bantered with Carl, the fourth, a man named Mac, flashed a malevolent glare at Terry. It was filled with so much hate that Terry felt he'd been physically accosted. Finally the four men admitted defeat and left, allowing the Bible-study group to continue their discussion.

On weeknights Terry headed for the lounge where the honor guardsmen gathered to swap their "battle" stories. Since he was still a JEEP and would be for his first eight months in the guard, he was eager to listen and learn.

"Remember the 'puddle pirate' who flaked, right on the White House lawn?" The men laughed as one of the old-timers told the embarrassing story of the coast guardsman who passed out while standing at attention. Like the coast guard term *puddle pirate*, each branch of the military sported a derogatory tag: army guardsmen were called "grunts"; navy, "squids"; marines, "jar heads"; and air force, "flyboys."

The old-timers loved to talk about the mistakes the other branches of the military had made and about encounters with famous people. Terry's favorite anecdotes involved the President himself. They all knew that a guardsman couldn't speak to the President unless the President spoke first, but President Reagan would speak to the members of the Honor Guard every now and then. These were the stories most treasured.

"Yeah, he's a real grandpa type, very relaxed—congenial," an old-timer explained. "He enjoys going out of his way to speak with the military personnel. It's awesome to stand face to face with one of the most powerful men in the world."

"Yeah," another said, "I always said that when I met him, I'd give him a piece of my mind over the tax increase on gasoline. Instead, I could barely answer his simplest questions."

Terry snorted to the JEEP sitting next to him. "Humph! I have a number of pertinent questions I'd ask him if I got the chance. For example—trading hostages for weapons." Anyone who knew Terry knew also how politically active Terry was. He had definite opinions on all the major issues and wasn't shy about expressing them.

One of his friends laughed and pounded Terry on the shoulder. "When he meets you, he'll think he ran into a black Geraldo Rivera."

The men hooted with laughter. "You wait," they cackled. "You'll wimp out just like the rest of us."

"Motor-mouth Johnson?" Carl wagged his finger at the doubters. "Never doubt Johnson's gift of gab. Take it from me, asleep or awake, he never stops. A simple encounter with the President of the United States won't slow him down."

Terry shrugged his shoulders. "What can I say? Guilty as charged."

Chapter Twenty

Sergeant Washington laughed at his friend's eagerness for an assignment, in spite of the boundaries put on their friendship. On duty Terry called him Sergeant Washington; off duty he was good old Reggie. "In time, Johnson, in time."

The hierarchy of guardsmen demanded that certain assignments carried with them more prestige than others. While an old-timer would be assigned a dinner at the White House, opening doors for or escorting senators' wives to their seats at D.C. social functions would go to a JEEP.

One morning, after returning from training at Arlington Cemetery, Terry and his roommate Carl climbed out of the bus and headed for the dormitory. They'd just entered the dormitory when Sergeant Washington called Terry into his office. "Hey, Johnson, you wanted an assignment. I've got one for you. Be ready tonight, in full dress uniform, at 1700 hours."

Terry's eyes danced with delight. A job, a real job! Up to this point all he'd done was practice routines and help carry a few caskets at funerals. This was his first real job not held in Arlington Cemetery.

"The Heritage Foundation is holding a $1,000-a-plate banquet tonight," Sergeant Washington explained. "Top military brass will be there, and they want the Honor Guard represented. Guards from the flag element will be there during the 'National Anthem.' Also, they need someone to man the door, and you're it."

"Yes, sir." Terry snapped off a salute. He whirled about and took long strides down the hallway toward his room. When he caught up with Carl, Terry told him about the dinner assignment. "Isn't that neat? I get to open—"

"Neat? It's a put-down." Carl snorted. "They'd only send a JEEP to do it."

"Well, that's what I am, right? I think it sounds like fun."

"Only you would." Carl grinned and shook his head. "Washington's just giving you busywork, something to keep you out of trouble until your Presidential clearance comes through. No one else would want to do it."

No one else would want to do it? A banquet in the Washington Hilton, and no one wants to go? Terry shook his head in wonder as he lined his neck scarf with cardboard and tied it into place. He put on his hat and carried his overblouse on a hanger out to the waiting bus. On the way to the hotel, Terry learned that the Heritage Foundation is a conservative and prestigious Republican social club in the Capitol area.

The guardsmen arrived at the Hilton long before the banquet was scheduled to start. Terry followed the more-experienced guardsmen, the flag bearers, into the hotel. As they passed through the outside doors, two men were assembling a piece of machinery on the stairsteps leading to the banquet hall.

Terry overheard one of the flag bearers ask his partner, "Why would they set up metal detectors here for a banquet?"

The second flag bearer snorted. "Who knows? Maybe the top brass invited to be here tonight are brassier than usual." The men swallowed their laughter when the evening's team leader strode toward them.

"Johnson, you stand here by the main entry to the banquet room. All you have to do is open the door whenever a guest approaches. Got it?"

Terry took a deep breath and snapped to attention. "Yes, sir!"

The team leader shook his head and mumbled, "Deliver me

from JEEPs and their enthusiasm."

Terry hadn't been at his post for more than fifteen minutes when a colonel approached. Terry smiled, saluted, and reached for the door handle.

The colonel paused and studied the guardsman for a moment. "You look like you're really enjoying your job, airman."

"Oh, yes, sir."

"Most guardsmen don't enjoy this job." The colonel eyed Terry a moment longer. "Come with me, son. I have a different assignment for you tonight."

Terry followed the colonel into the banquet hall. They walked to the front of the carefully appointed dining hall and over to a door on the right of the dais. "You stand here at this door. I'll be on the other side of the dais on a walkie-talkie. When I give the signal, you open the door."

"Yes, sir." Terry nodded and took his place beside the door. Terry enjoyed the action inside the banquet hall more than he had standing out in the hallway. An arrogant and fastidious *maître d'hôtel* in a black tuxedo rushed about the room, giving a stream of commands to anyone within hearing range of his voice. Waiters in tuxedos with shorter cropped jackets and cummerbunds scurried about the tables, adjusting centerpieces and filling water goblets to the satisfaction of the little martinet. Musicians entered the banquet room wearing expressions ranging from brisk efficiency to boredom. They took their places in the orchestra pit and tuned their instruments, ready to begin playing when the first guests entered. Terry still couldn't believe his luck at being chosen for this assignment, regardless of what Carl and the others said.

He watched as the first of the guests arrived. Another guardsman had been assigned to replace him at the main entrance. The flow of guests arriving increased with the importance of the guest and the nearness of the hour for the banquet to begin. Congressmen and their spouses, military generals from all five branches of the service and their spouses, cabinet members and other distinguished heads of state and their spouses entered regally, bearing the importance of their positions as they walked to their assigned places at the tables. Terry's pulse raced as he recognized many of the faces from the news interviews he'd watched on television and from newspaper photographs. Every few seconds, he glanced over at the colonel, whose attention seemed divided between men wearing dark business suits and the electronic box cupped in his hand.

As the last of the guests were escorted to their tables, Terry glanced over at the colonel, whose head was bowed over his radio. He had no idea what congressman or general would be on the other side of the door. Terry wrapped his white gloved fingers around the brass door handle as the colonel lifted his head and marked time like a band director: 3-2-1. On the signal, Terry clicked his heels together in proper military fashion and saluted the arriving dignitary. He held the salute for a stunned second as his mouth dropped open, and his eyes bugged out at the sight of his smiling commander in chief, President Reagan.

In unison, the audience rose to their feet. Terry failed to hear the band's majestic strains of "Hail to the Chief" or see the reporters' cameras flash in rapid succession before his face. Instead his mind raced ahead in panic. I'm not supposed to be here, he thought. I don't have presidential clearance yet. And this is definitely President Reagan!

President Reagan paused in front of Terry and gave him a broad, friendly smile. "How are you doing tonight, airman? How are you doing?"

Terry's famous motor-mouth confidence shifted into reverse. His brain grounded to a four-wheel-drive stop. When he tried to reply to the President's question, all he could get out was a string of unintelligible babble. "I ba-ba-ba-ba-ba-ba."

The President's eyes twinkled as he cast a wry grin at Terry, then turned toward the aide following him, "I guess he's a little nervous." The aide chuckled, then escorted the bemused President Reagan up to the platform.

Once he reached center stage, the President waved to his surprised and adoring supporters, acknowledging special individual guests with a nod or the thumbs-up gesture until the music and the applause died down. Cameras continued to flash as he spoke with his famous, easygoing California drawl. He told the guests how he had decided to attend the banquet only thirty minutes before it was scheduled to begin.

Midway through his prepared speech, Reagan stopped speaking and looked down at his notes for several seconds as if he'd lost his concentration. A good-natured grin formed at the corners of his mouth as he shook his head. ". . . that airman at the door . . ."

Terry blushed as the audience turned to locate the source of the President's amusement. With all the noise and surprise caused by the President's unexpected arrival, few guests had caught the exchange between the President and the young airman.

Terry steeled himself against the razzing he'd get from his friends when he got back to Bolling that night, and his colleagues didn't disappoint him. One of the traits they most admired about him was his ability to laugh at himself. He took both his successes and failures in the same relaxed style.

His circle of friends grew, and as the circle grew, so did the newly organized Bible-study group. However, not everyone liked the good-natured northwesterner. No matter how hard Terry tried, he couldn't break through one particular guardsman's wall of hate. Terry scoured his brain trying to determine what he could possibly have done to offend Mac. Even before he qualified for the Honor Guard, Terry recalled seeing Mac and his friends walk past his room on Friday nights while the group was studying the Bible. The evil glare Mac would cast at Terry made him feel as if he needed to scrub off a greasy film of hate. Then Mac would shake his head and leave. Mac's hostility intensified with each additional encounter.

At first Terry surmised that Mac's problem had something to do with racial prejudice, but somehow, the man's hatred seemed much more intense than that. Frustrated with the situation, Terry cornered Sam. The man had roomed with Mac for a short time.

"I don't understand it. No matter how I try, I can't get through to that guy. Does he hate blacks so much?"

Sam studied his hands for a few seconds before speaking. "No, at least I don't think so."

"Well, then, what is it? Have I done something to offend him?"

The ex-roommate hesitated, nervously scraping his thumbnail against his pinky nail. "The only offense you've committed is holding your Bible studies."

"I-I-I don't understand."

"The man's a Satanist!" Sam spoke the words with surprising vehemence. "He hates you because you're a Christian."

Terry rolled his eyes incredulously. "Come on, a Satanist?"

"Why do you think I moved out of the room after only two weeks as his roommate? The guy's a nut case. He holds secret satanic meetings at midnight, black candles and all."

"Right!" Terry chuckled nervously. This is crazy, he thought, a bunch of nonsense!

Sam smiled as if he could read Terry's mind. "You laugh, but you are his main target. He's obsessed with you. He writes your name in ashes and waves what he calls his sacred magic wand over it while babbling a bunch of nonsense."

Terry shot Sam a skeptical look. No person in his right mind would believe such nonsense.

"Go ahead and doubt, but I'm telling you the truth. It was enough to scare the liver out of me, I'll tell you that." Sam's voice dropped to a whisper. "He keeps baby spiders in his room to use for his sacrifices. And he says he's going to buy some snakes, since snakes have more power against Christians than spiders."

A cold draft of fear swept through Terry's body. He'd heard stories about voodoo and black magic; he shivered, then tried to recover his bravado. "I've never heard anything so ridiculous!"

"Look, you asked me, and I told you. That's all I can say." Sam shrugged and walked away.

Terry returned to his room and dropped to his knees beside his bed. "Is Sam telling the truth, Lord? It sounds about as likely as a story line from 'Star Trek.'" After praying a short prayer for wisdom, he rose from his knees and walked over to his desk, where his Bible lay open. "If what Sam says is true, Father, I'm scared. Please help me. I've never faced honest-to-goodness devils before."

He picked up his Bible and opened it to the book of Luke and began reading. When he finished chapter 9, he continued on to 10. The words of verse 17 leaped out at him. "Even the devils are subject unto us through thy name." Terry read verses 19 and 20. "Behold, I give unto you power to tread on serpents and scorpions, and over all the power of the enemy: and nothing shall by any means hurt you. Notwithstanding in this rejoice not, that the spirits are subject unto you; but rather rejoice, because your names are written in heaven."

He read the verses again. He could hardly believe it. A promise so exact had been in his Bible all along just waiting for the moment when he would need it most.

Three weeks later, Sergeant Washington called Terry to his office to tell him that Mac had been discharged from the Honor Guard for practicing satanic rituals. "I'm telling you this as a Christian brother, not as your sergeant, because Mac's evil curses were directed almost solely against you."

Chapter Twenty-one

Terry rubbed his forehead and groaned. Staring down at the black letters typed on the white test sheet brought back memories he preferred to forget. "Get used to it. You'll take a lot more tests when you start college after leaving the military," he mumbled to himself. "Besides, it's just a plain old vocabulary test like Mrs. Winter used to give back at the academy." He searched the page for the spot where he'd left off.

When Terry saw the announcement on the bulletin board offering evening reading classes, he decided to attend. He knew his parents had been praying about his reading problem for years. Maybe this was the perfect time to do something about it, he thought. He took the class, but when it came to the examination, Terry felt the same trauma he'd experienced so many times during his grade-school and academy years even before he walked into the room. The female examiner, a tall, congenial blond sergeant in her late thirties, tried to ease his nervousness.

"Don't let the tests throw you, airman. You managed to pass all the tests for getting into the United States Air Force. Those were the difficult ones, not these."

"Yes, ma'am." Terry stared at the page in front of him once more. The words might as well have been Russian for all he could tell. A cold sweat trickled down his neck as he penciled in his answers. At the bottom of the page, he heaved a sigh and handed the answer sheet to the woman.

Terry watched as she ran her pencil down his list of answers, checking off first one problem, then another. After counting the check marks, she looked up at him.

"Man." She whistled through her teeth. "Your parents must have spent a whole lot of money on you. Your tutor must have been outstanding."

"What tutor?"

"The one who helped you with your dyslexia." She paused and studied his test sheet again. "Must have been a genius."

Terry frowned. "Dyslexia? What dyslexia?"

Continuing as if she hadn't heard his question, she said, "I think you might be the first disabled or handicapped person ever to be in the President's Honor Guard."

Handicapped? Disabled? Terry thought. What is she talking about?

Looking over the rim of her glasses, she said, "Don't you know that you have dyslexia in the third degree? I don't know how in the world you passed your air force admissions, let alone the psychological and military aptitude tests—there's no way!"

"I have what?"

She cleared her throat. "Isn't it a little harder for you to read and spell?"

Terry's mind flashed back to Mrs. Pennyworth's classroom. "Yes, ma'am."

"It's because you have dyslexia, a reading disorder. You must have had some of the best tutors around. For a person with your degree of dyslexia, you have reached the point where it's almost undetectable." The woman leaned her elbow on the desktop and flipped through his cumulative folder.

Terry thought back through his childhood—first grade, second, third, and on through high school. "As far as I know, I've never had a tutor in my entire life."

"You just don't remember." She smiled and shook her head. "There is no way in the world you could have passed all the air force examinations, especially without at least two years of college classwork."

"My parents have been praying about my lack of reading

skills for years, and I know that Jesus has helped me with my reading problem." Terry thought for a moment. "Otherwise, I didn't even know I had this dyslexia thing."

At the mention of Jesus, the examiner's eyes glassed over with disinterest as if her mind was folding into itself.

He continued explaining. "Back in high school I did have an English teacher, Mrs. Winter, who took an interest in me. When I started having trouble in her classes, she kept me after class and told me that if I wanted to improve my reading I should read aloud a chapter from the Bible every night until I could read it perfectly. And when I came upon a word I didn't know, I should go back to it and write it down."

"I don't believe it," she muttered as she started at the front of the file for a third time. "There must be some record here of a specially trained tutor or coach somewhere."

"There was Mrs. Winter's granddaughter, Tracy. She helped me with my reading a few times after school."

"No, no, that wouldn't do it. Your making such progress would have taken years of intensified training." Again the examiner shook her head. "The Bible?"

"The Bible." Terry grinned. "Let me tell you a little about myself." He told her about his childhood and his experiences since joining the military. He told her how he'd given his life to Christ and how God had perfectly timed each setback and used it for good. "Considering all that He's done for me, I have no problem accepting the possibility that Jesus and His Word have been my tutors all along." After he told his story, he left the classroom, never to meet the woman again and not knowing whether she believed his incredible story.

Dyslexia! No wonder he had had problems learning to read! With dyslexia, the messages between people's eyes and their brains are somehow scrambled, so that often they see words or letters backward. By no means unintelligent, dyslexics are often underachievers because their brains simply don't process things correctly.

It did explain why Mrs. Pennyworth and the others considered him retarded. It might even explain some of his difficulties marching and aiming a rifle. Terry shook his head.

"And God helped me overcome this disability I didn't even know I had."

A brisk autumn breeze whipped over the hillside of white crosses as the Honor Guard unit drew to attention over the casket of an air force general, a hero from World War II. Terry moved through the routine with practiced ease. The mourners, the general's daughter and son-in-law, stood on each side of the veiled widow, supporting her in her grief. Three teenagers, ill at ease and uncertain about the protocol, waited off to one side throughout the flag-folding ceremony.

Terry remembered the pain he'd felt standing beside his mother when his father died. He fought down the familiar wave of homesickness once more. This would be the first Thanksgiving and Christmas he'd ever spent away from his family.

Since the weeks between Thanksgiving and New Year's Eve were the busiest of all the year for the Honor Guard, only half of the men were allowed to leave at any one time—one-half at Thanksgiving, the other at Christmas. Cost and distance forced Terry to be realistic. Other men had to make the same less-than-cheerful sacrifice of not going home at all.

The men left behind spent their evenings off duty in front of the television complaining. Tempers flared. While the mess hall crew prepared special foods and strung decorations throughout the dining hall, it wasn't home for the lonely men.

One night, after spending the evening listening to everyone gripe and snarl at one another, Terry lay in the dark feeling totally alone and more miserable than he'd ever felt before. Suddenly he remembered how Elder Matula organized the students to go out and help people in the community. If an elderly woman needed someone to mow her lawn, students would do it. If someone needed a porch railing fixed, the high-school kids volunteered. The teacher told the students that there was always someone who was worse off than they and who could use a little help. Elder Matula insisted that during the holidays volunteer agencies could use all the help they could get. That's what we need, Terry thought, to think about someone worse off than ourselves.

The next morning, he went to see Sergeant Washington. "I gotta get out of here. I'm going stir-crazy. Do you know of any agencies that feed the homeless on Thanksgiving?"

Sergeant Washington thought for a moment. "I can't think of any off hand, but I do know that the Georgetown University Hospital feeds the senior citizens of the community every Thanksgiving."

Terry thanked his friend and found the hospital's number in the telephone book. He called and asked to talk with the head of volunteer services. After identifying himself as a member of the President's Honor Guard, he explained how he and a few of his buddies were stuck on base for the holidays. "I heard about your program, and I was wondering if you could use a little help on Thanksgiving Day."

The volunteer coordinator eagerly accepted the airman's offer. When Terry got off the phone, he posted a sign on the dormitory bulletin board. "Instead of griping about your problems, why not help someone else? Sign up to help feed the senior citizens of Georgetown on Thanksgiving Day."

Chapter Twenty-two

The eager volunteers climbed aboard the bus for the Georgetown Hospital on Thanksgiving morning. Terry read the list, checking off names as he went. He turned to the driver. "All present and accounted for. Let's roll." If anyone had told him when he first posted the sign-up sheet that so many of the guardsmen would volunteer, he would never have believed it. After all, no one listened to a JEEP. Five, maybe ten volunteers, yes, but thirty? Maybe I've stumbled onto something here, he thought. Maybe other guardsmen feel cramped by the closed community the Honor Guard system fosters. What a neat way to witness both to the men and to the people we help!

He tucked the thought into a back pocket of his mind and stared at the world of browns and grays beyond his window. Even the Potomac River flowed muddy brown from the heavy autumn rains. A wave of loneliness flitted across his mind when he thought of the grove of massive, deep green Douglas firs across the street from his mother's home and the lawns and fields that would still be a rich Oregon green.

"Hey, Johnson." One volunteer pulled his thoughts back to the present. "How late do you think we'll stay?"

"I guess until they don't need us any longer."

When the bus stopped in front of the Georgetown Hospital, a committee of community volunteers welcomed the guardsmen. The hospital cafeteria sported orange, yellow, and brown streamers festooned with the traditional turkey-and-pilgrim motif. A softly padded, take-charge matron with overpermed and overteased red hair barked out orders like a seasoned basic training instructor. "You boys, in the kitchen, peeling potatoes. You, you, and you, set up tables and chairs. You four, follow me."

Whether it was peeling, whipping, beating, chopping, or stuffing, the volunteers attacked each assignment with enthusiasm and good humor. During a break before the guests arrived, a senior airman grating carrots across the deck from Terry said, "When I think of all the football games my father, brothers, and I enjoyed while my mother stood in the kitchen peeling potatoes, I'm ashamed! I will never take her Thanksgiving dinner for granted again."

"That's for sure," Terry admitted as he cut a slippery cucumber into thin strips.

The delightful aromas of roast turkey, bubbling brown gravy, candied sweet potatoes, and freshly baked pumpkin pies filled the hospital cafeteria and beyond. Volcanoes of mashed potatoes with melted butter dripping down the slopes; the rich burgundy-colored cranberry sauce; and trays of pickles, olives, and fresh vegetables provided a feast for the eye.

The coordinator scanned the dining hall, adjusted the centerpiece on the serving table, and waved her palm toward the main entrance. "Open the doors, gentlemen. Our guests have arrived."

Tears misted in Terry's eyes as he stepped back to watch smiling guardsmen mingle with the delighted guests, helping those who needed assistance with trays and wheeling wheelchairs through the serving lines. Men who'd just hours before been surly and nasty with one another cheerfully ran a shuttle back and forth to the kitchen restocking the serving deck. Others, with the sleeves of their air force fatigues rolled up over bulging muscles, stood over hot suds rinsing food scraps off dirty platters before loading them into the dishwasher.

The coordinator bustled between the kitchen and dining room with efficient ease. "Airman Johnson," she whispered as she passed Terry's station, "I don't know how we ever did this without you and your friends."

After the last dish was washed, dried, and stacked on the shelves, after the last pan was scrubbed to a military shine, the hospital volunteers and the guardsmen sighed with uniform relief. With obvious reluctance, the exhausted guardsmen waved goodbye to their new friends and staggered onto the bus for the short ride back to their dormitory. Muscles ached by the time they arrived back at the dormitory and climbed down off the bus.

One of the men slapped Terry on his shoulder as they entered the building. "I've never been so beat in all my life! I may never be able to look a mashed Idaho potato in the eye again. Thanks for inviting me along; I had a great time."

A second guard added, "I never realized how neat old people can be. I met a woman who's related to Pocahontas—can you imagine? Pocahontas!"

Terry waved good night to the other men and hurried to his room, where he grabbed his toiletries and headed to the shower. He groaned with pleasure as the hot spray pelted the knotted muscles in his shoulder and back. He thought back over the day. The hospital personnel had repeated over and over again how impressed they were with the men's willingness to help. He was surprised to realize he'd gone the entire day without feeling homesick. He finished his shower, wrapped the towel around his hips, and headed down the hall toward his room.

"Hey, Johnson." The Honor Guard's worst complainer stuck his head out of his room. "What are we going to do on Christmas Day?"

Terry turned, expecting to see a sneer on the man's face; instead, the man glowed with excitement. "Uh, well, I'll let you know in a day or two." What a way to reach people, he thought. Why not use the Honor Guard for volunteer charity work?

During the days before Christmas, he found a number of community projects wanting and needing volunteers. He arranged with the St. Andrews Catholic Church to have the guardsmen help collect food for its annual can drive. When the first team of guardsmen returned from their holiday leave, they got into the program as well. A spirit of family developed among the men.

Yet when Christmas Eve arrived, and most of the men had either gone to visit relatives or gone partying, that old familiar ache of loneliness set in for Terry. Rather than sit around the dormitory and mope, he rented a car. At least I can drive around and enjoy the Christmas lights, he thought.

By the time he picked up his rental car at the agency, the downtown traffic had thinned out. Strings of multicolored lights scalloped across the streets as he headed northeast through the city. The blinking lights reflected off the hood and windshield of the rental car. Driving down a street where every home was decorated reminded him of the times he and his family had walked along the famous Peacock Street in Portland on Christmas Eve to admire the lighted homes. He turned the knob on the car radio. Instantly, Robert Goulet's rendition of "O Come, All Ye Faithful" filled the automobile.

The streets grew emptier with each block. Having nowhere definite in mind, he turned first down one block, then another, until he came upon a street clogged with vehicles and people. Hmmm, I wonder where everyone's going, he thought. He maneuvered the car into a parking space, then headed back to where he'd first seen all the people.

He heard the Christmas carols before he saw the crowd gathered outside what appeared to be a school. He read the sign "Takoma Academy" on the lawn and thought for a moment. I didn't know schools other than Adventist ones used *academy* in their names. He craned his neck to see what was happening at the front of the crowd. A Christmas pageant, complete with live animals. I don't believe it, he thought. He maneuvered his way toward the front for a better view.

Enraptured by the scene, Terry allowed the age-old story to carry him back in time to the birth of Christ. He no longer felt homesick or lonely. In this group of celebrating Christians, he knew he was at home. And to complete the mood of holiday joy, soft, lazy snowflakes began falling as the audience joined the actors to sing the carol "Silent Night."

A craggy-faced older man wearing a heavy woolen cap and

a plaid muffler about his throat tapped Terry on the shoulder as he turned to leave. The man introduced himself. They talked for a few minutes about how Terry just happened upon the celebration.

"I noticed the sign back there. Just what kind of school is Takoma Academy, anyway?" Terry asked.

The stranger smiled. "Oh, Takoma Academy is a co-educational high school run by the Seventh-day Adventist Church."

Terry's mouth dropped open. "I-I'm a Seventh-day Adventist. I graduated from Portland Adventist Academy."

The man grabbed Terry's hand and pumped it enthusiastically. "Imagine that! Can you imagine that!"

On the way back to base, Terry thought, How can I complain of homesickness when God arranged for my eternal family to help fill my loneliness for my physical family back in Oregon?

Soon after the first of the year, Sergeant Washington stopped Terry in the dormitory hallway. "Terry, the Honor Guard commander wants to see you right away."

"Right, sir." Terry hurried to the commander's office, where the commander's personal secretary ushered him in immediately to see the commander.

"At ease, Johnson." The commander arose and came around his massive oak desk to where Terry stood. "Young man, I want to shake your hand." He pumped Terry's hand enthusiastically. "You are to be commended. You have brought the United States Air Force Honor Guard more good PR in four weeks than most guardsmen contribute throughout their entire service in the unit."

Terry swallowed hard. "Thank you, sir."

The commander indicated that Terry should sit down. "I have received a flood of letters from Georgetown Hospital personnel, from Washington, D.C., Catholic diocese, from the military brass, and even from the mayor's office commending you for your volunteer efforts during the holidays."

"But, sir, there were plenty others who—"

"No modesty, my boy. I talked with Sergeant Washington.

He told me that you were the catalyst." The commander shook his head and glanced out the window onto the drizzle of the day. "Such a simple idea—volunteer work. Why couldn't our public relations office have thought of it? If you come up with any more ideas, let me know."

In the months that followed, the community response for the Honor Guard's ongoing involvement in local fund-raisers, walk-a-thons, and other events drew more attention from the top air force officials. Hardly a month went by, but Terry received a personal letter of thank-you or an official letter of commendation for his permanent file. While the recommendations accumulating in his file would go toward future promotions, the chance to witness excited Terry more. He knew he would never become a career man in the air force, but he would always be in the service of his Lord. All the preaching he could have done would never have been as unifying or as far-reaching as was the witness of doing.

Chapter Twenty-three

On January 28, Terry and his friends wolfed down their breakfasts and rushed back to the dormitory for morning inspection. Sergeant Washington went through the motions as quickly as possible. No one wanted to miss a moment of the media event of the decade. When the sergeant completed morning inspection, the men charged down the hall and into the lounge to reserve their places in front of the wide-screened TV. By the time the network anchor appeared on camera, there was standing room along the back wall only.

"It's a bitterly cold morning here at the Kennedy Space Center. The early-morning liftoff of the space shuttle *Challenger* has been postponed once again." Shots of tourists sharing thermoses of hot coffee with each other and eating doughnuts and of kids waving flags and making faces in front of the live video camera flashed on the screen as the smoothly coiffured anchor continued. "The crew were briefed of the delay at breakfast but are expected to board momentarily. There is still hope that liftoff might be possible later on."

A groan passed through the Honor Guard lounge. "Another delay! I'm gonna go get a cup of coffee. Save my place."

The TV anchor turned the narration over to a smiling blond reporter standing in front of the VIP spectator bleachers. Exhaling clouds of vapor into the frigid air, she identified each of the people shivering in the icy morning air.

Sitting on the floor beside Terry, Carl shuddered. "Boy, it makes me cold just watching them on television."

The TV cameras focused on a second reporter. Behind him the black-and-white orbiter gleamed in the cool winter sunlight on Pad 39B. "NASA's mission management team is concerned about the sheets of ice and icicles around the launch pad."

Throughout the morning, the guardsmen, along with millions of other Americans, huddled around their television, ready to cheer their country on. As members of the air force, the guardsmen felt an even stronger bond of loyalty for the mission.

The laughing faces of the orbiter crew boarding the space bus flashed on the television screen, followed by the official portrait. The anchor read off their names as the camera focused on each face: physicist and mission specialist, Ellison Onizuka; pilot, Mike Smith; teacher, Christa McAuliffe; mission commander, Dick Scobee; engineer, Greg Jarvis; mission specialist and electrical engineer, Judy Resnik; and mission specialist and physicist, Ron McNair.

Countdown began at 11:00 a.m. When it stopped at T minus nine minutes to allow technicians to assess the problem of ice forming on the shell of the shuttle, the entire room of guardsmen groaned. The anchor reflected the same impatience many NASA officials had expressed during the previous postponements. In the months previous to the day's mission, NASA's public relations department had worked hard to build up the country's interest in space flight once again. Now they feared the delays would scuttle the momentum they'd developed.

A cheer went up in the Honor Guard lounge when the technicians decided at 11:15 there was no danger, and the NASA control room announced that the countdown would recommence at 11:29, setting the actual liftoff at 11:38.

Tensions around the nation grew at T minus six seconds, when the high whine of the main engines began, deepening into a deafening roar, followed by the blast from the two solid-fuel rocket boosters. The *Challenger* rose out of dramatic clouds of billowing smoke and steam followed by a tail of fire.

Cries of "All right!" and "Go for it!" filled the lounge and the television screen as the shuttle passed through the sound barrier. The sequence of events that followed would be televised for days to come, when the *Challenger* suddenly exploded into a billowing cloud and a whirling ball of fire. Thin trails of steam swirled to the earth. People around the world watched in stunned silence as the shuttle disintegrated into a thousand pieces of scrap metal.

Terry stared in the direction of the television, neither hearing nor seeing further news coverage. One minute, seven people faced the adventure of a lifetime; and the next moment, eternity. Slowly, as if moving through a distorted dream sequence, Terry rose to his feet. Others around him were doing the same thing. No one seemed aware of his surroundings.

"I need some air," he mumbled, stumbling past a couple of airmen still seated near the doorway. Grabbing his topcoat from his locker, Terry rushed out into the bitter January temperatures. "Run," a voice inside his brain prompted, "run!" Minutes later, chattering teeth and a cold, stinging face forced him to return to the dormitory.

That evening the guardsmen filled the lounge once again to watch their commander in chief, wan and shaken, speak to a nation in mourning. His speech included these words of condolence: "Nothing ends here. Our hopes and our journeys continue."

Terry rifled through a mass of mixed emotions the next morning when he learned he'd been selected to be in charge of crowd control at USAF Commander Scobee's funeral at Arlington National Cemetery. On the day of the funeral, the guardsmen assigned to carry the empty casket ascended the hill to the grave site, behind the amphitheater for the Tomb of the Unknown Soldier, a spot specially chosen for the members of the *Challenger* tragedy. Terry walked closer to the rear of the casket, making certain that reporters and photographers didn't press too close to either the casket or the mourners.

Terry felt his heart tug as he scanned the drawn faces of the mourners. When tears threatened to rise, he shifted his attention back to the media crew. He had learned during his few short months with the Honor Guard that to control the natural flow of emotions at these funerals, he needed to concentrate on his assigned task instead of focusing on the pain registered in faces of the deceased's loved ones.

His self-control worked until Commander Scobee's brother stood and lifted his bugle to his lips. As the first few notes of taps rang out over the silent hillside, Terry refused to look toward the family members still seated. He had to keep swallowing in order to maintain proper decorum. But when the notes of the bugle broke halfway through the song, Terry struggled unsuccessfully to choke back the tears. He glanced toward his fellow guardsmen to see if they'd noticed his breach of military behavior. He needn't have worried. Tears streamed down the men's faces unchecked. The sudden movement of an overzealous news photographer forced Terry's thoughts back to his assigned task, allowing him to regain control of his emotions.

Chapter Twenty-four

January's arctic winds whipped across the base as Terry hurried into the dormitory. He dropped off his topcoat in his locker and hurried into the recreation room, where a number of off-duty guardsmen had gathered. A loud voice by the television caught Terry's attention. He wandered closer to discover what might be happening.

In the middle of the group, a frustrated airman scanned the circle of closed faces. "I don't know what I'm going to do! Please, won't someone cover my Saturday-night assignment?"

One of the men scoffed. "Rob, you've got to be kidding! Give up a Saturday night in Georgetown for an insignificant little dinner party?"

"Look, I'm best man at Al Nelson's wedding that night!" Rob folded his hands and pleaded with his friends. Al Nelson, a senior guardsman, carried the presidential colors directly behind the President. "Won't any of you help me out?"

Terry ambled over to the cluster of guardsmen. "Help? I'll help you. How can I help?"

The men burst out laughing. The JEEP's reputation for always volunteering was a source of both admiration and humor. "Yeah," one of the men gestured toward Terry, "the new guy will help you, won't you, Johnson?"

Rob turned toward Terry, his eyes filled with hope. He explained the Saturday-night assignment to Terry. "So you see, it's not much at all."

"No problem. I'll be glad to take your place."

"Are you serious?" He whipped out his checkbook and pen lest Terry change his mind. "How much will I have to pay you? Fifty bucks?" Fifty to sixty dollars was the going rate for taking another man's shift.

"No." Terry shook his head.

"All right, sixty, then."

"I said No." Terry laughed out loud. "I'm not going to charge you anything."

Rob stared in disbelief. "Are you serious? You're really not going to charge me?"

Terry walked over to an end table and picked up a copy of the daily newspaper. "Of course not. I'm glad to do it. You need to get to your friend's wedding, and I don't have anything better to do on Saturday night."

Rob followed him across the room. "I'll remember this, Johnson." Terry smiled and opened the paper.

"You could always get a girl, Johnson," one of the other men razzed. "Then you'd have better things to do with your Saturday nights."

Terry peered over the top of the paper and grinned. "Don't you worry about me, Sanders. I do just fine in that department." Terry had decided before joining the military to postpone all romantic involvements until he returned to college.

"Come on, even a one-night stand is better than nothing," Sanders continued.

"No thanks, guys. That's not my style." He returned to his reading. After a few minutes the men lost interest in harassing him.

The Monday after the wedding, Rob fell into step beside Terry as he headed to breakfast. "Hey, thanks again, man, for covering for me on Saturday night. Did everything go all right?"

"What's to go wrong escorting senators' wives to their seats?"

"If you ask that question, obviously you are still a JEEP."

When Al Nelson returned from his honeymoon, he hunted up the JEEP who "saved his wedding." "Sandy and I want to thank you in a special way," Al explained. "I understand you're a Christian. Well, so are we, and we'd like to invite you to church with us next Sunday, then over to our apartment for Sunday dinner."

Terry's eyes lighted up with pleasure. The thought of a genuine home-cooked meal sounded terrific. Then he hesitated. "Isn't it a little unusual for an old-timer to socialize with a JEEP?"

Al laughed. "Probably so, but Sandy and I were so impressed with your generosity, we wanted to say thanks. And a home-cooked meal seemed like a good idea."

"I can't think of anything I'd enjoy more."

"Great." Al nodded. "I'll pick you up at 8:30 on Sunday morning."

On Sunday morning, Al's Pontiac LE pulled up in front of the dormitory right on schedule. Terry walked to the car and got in. "Where's Sandy?"

"Oh, we're going to pick her up on the way to church. She's so worried about this meal. It's the first she's made since we got married, and she wants everything to be perfect."

"You're kidding. Wouldn't you two rather enjoy it alone without a third person?"

Al waved to the guard at the gate and drove on. "Oh, no, she's eager to meet you. She already dumped her tomato aspic down the garbage disposal because it didn't look exactly the way she wanted it to look."

When they pulled up in front of the apartment house where the Nelsons lived, a sassy-looking redhead waved from the upstairs window and within seconds rushed out the front door and down the steps to the car.

"I'll get the door." Terry hopped out of the automobile and opened the front door for her.

"Hi." Her eyes sparkled with happiness. "I'm Sandy. And you're Terry, right?"

"Nice to meet you, Sandy. I really appreciate this invitation." Terry closed her door, then climbed into the back seat.

They laughed and talked all the way to the church. By the time they parked in the parking lot of a popular church in the area, Terry felt he'd known Al and Sandy for a long time. The church members welcomed him with the same spontaneous grace.

On the way back to the apartment, Al glanced back at Terry. "So how did you like the sermon?"

"Yeah," Sandy added, "doesn't Reverend Neff preach well?"

Terry thought for a moment. "He is very sincere in what he believes, I can tell."

Al eyed Terry in the rearview mirror. "Well, what do you think about his theory that everyone is going to be saved? That there is no literal hell, for instance?"

Here's one to test your diplomacy, Terry told himself. "I guess I interpret the Bible a little differently on that particular point. There are so many traditions and customs that have slipped into the churches, Catholic and Protestant alike, that I feel a need to get back to the basics of the Bible and the beliefs of the early Christian church."

Sandy turned around, her forehead knitted into a question. "Like what?"

Terry started to answer, when Al brought the Pontiac to a stop in front of their apartment house. "Oh, oh," Sandy interrupted, hopping out of the car before either man could open her door. "It will have to wait at least until dinner is served."

They climbed the stairs to the one-bedroom apartment. Terry smiled to himself as he glanced about the light and airy living room. It felt good to be in an honest-to-goodness home again instead of a dorm room.

"Let me take your coat." Al took Terry's coat and hung it in the hall closet. "Just make yourself at home. Sandy says dinner will be ready in just a couple minutes." Al reentered the parlor and sank into a giant overstuffed club chair. "And she says that we're not to continue where we left off in the car until she can hear everything you have to say."

"Fine with me. Is there anything I can do to help?" Terry volunteered.

"Are you kidding? Neither of us is allowed within ten feet of that kitchen right now."

The two men talked about life in the Honor Guard for a few minutes. Al entertained Terry with some of his Honor Guard anecdotes.

With the grace of one of Washington's finest hostesses, Sandy glided into the room. "Dinner is served, gentlemen."

Terry followed the young couple into the dining room. A snowy white linen tablecloth draped the rectangular table. Two white candles in a set of crystal holders sat on each side of a floral centerpiece. Crystal water goblets and brand-new sterling silverware graced each setting, along with matching white linen table napkins.

Al kissed his bride on the neck, then turned to Terry. "I told you she intended to do this right."

Terry smiled at his expectant hostess. "Sandy, you have set a beautiful table."

"Thanks." She gave a nervous giggle. "Now, if only the food turns out half as well as the table settings."

"I'm sure everything will be perfect," her young husband assured her as he took his place across from Terry.

Once her guest and her husband were settled, Sandy bustled from the room, then back again, carrying the main course and side dishes, artistically arranged on her wedding china. She placed one plate in front of Terry and the other in front of Al. "You two go ahead and start eating without me. I need to add the finishing touches to our dessert."

Terry stared down at the plate of food in front of him and swallowed hard. Potatoes au gratin, green beans, creamed corn, and a giant, perfectly browned pork chop. He looked toward the kitchen, then back down at his plate. Sweat beaded on his forehead. What shall I do? he thought. I can't insult Sandy by not eating it, but . . . he had never eaten pork before, and the very thought of eating it turned his stomach. When Terry didn't begin eating right away, his host whispered, "Is something the matter?"

Terry looked at Al, then back down again at the pork chop, then up again at his host. "I-I-I don't quite know how to say this, but I don't think I can—"

Al peered at Terry's plate, trying to determine what the problem might be. "The potatoes? The corn—what's wrong?"

"The pork chop . . . I, uh—" Terry gulped. "Would you like it?"

Al frowned, took the chop, ate the meat quickly, and returned the bone to Terry's plate before Sandy returned to the room.

Later, as they talked about the morning's sermon, Terry mentioned that he was a Seventh-day Adventist.

"Oh, then you don't eat pork," Sandy exclaimed. "Why didn't you say something? My boss is a Seventh-day Adventist. I really admire her."

A look of guilt passed between her husband and Terry.

Sandy folded her hands and glared. "OK, what's up with you two?"

Al wrinkled his face with dread. "Terry didn't want to make you feel bad, so, well, I ate it."

Sandy stared in amazement. "Yours and his too?" Al and Terry glanced at one another, then back at Sandy and nodded. Sandy giggled and shook her head. "You two look like you've just been caught with your hands in the proverbial cookie jar."

The relaxed atmosphere continued while Terry answered their questions about the Bible and the discrepancies in the modern church. When Al dropped Terry off at the dormitory that evening, he said, "Would it be possible to get together again and talk? I would love to know the Bible as well as you do."

Terry smiled. "Sure, but remember, I have lots to learn myself. Let's set a time we can meet each week and study the Bible together."

They agreed on a time, and Al drove off. Terry took the steps into the dormitory three at a time. He threw the door of his room open, stepped inside, and closed it behind him. He leaned back against the door and lifted his arms in victory. "Yes! Yes! Thank You, Father."

Chapter Twenty-five

Winter passed in a string of State Department banquets and White House receptions for visiting foreign dignitaries. The cherry trees along the tidal basin blossomed and sprouted leaves. Standing at attention during a funeral service at Arlington National Cemetery or walking beside a caisson carrying a casket was much more comfortable once the winds sweeping up the grassy hillside from the Potomac River warmed.

The weekly meetings with Al and Sandy continued, even after the couple began attending church with her boss's family. When Sandy became pregnant, Terry felt like a proud uncle.

One evening, when Al picked up Terry for a Bible study, Terry noticed how drawn his friend looked. "Hey, what's up, man? You look like death warmed over."

"Sorry." Al muttered. "I just received an overseas assignment, which means I won't see Sandy for at least a year and a half. The baby will be at least eight months old before I get to see it."

"That's a tough break, man." Terry thought for a few minutes. "But you haven't shipped over yet. It's not hopeless."

Al shook his head in disbelief. "It's impossible. I put in a request, but you know the military."

"Hey, have you forgotten all the doors God opened for me since I joined the air force? If He can open doors for me, wait until you see what He does for you."

The three prayed together each week that God would re-route Al's orders for stateside in a community where they could find a friendly church in which to worship. As the time approached for Al to leave, Terry met with them each evening to pray together.

Seven days before he was to ship out, Al burst into Terry's room at the dormitory. "Johnson! Johnson, you're not going to believe this, but my orders have been changed to Maine, of all places, if Sandy and I can be ready to leave in three days!"

Terry pounded Al on the back. "He did it! I'll be over tomorrow night to help you all pack. After all, we don't want Sandy to get overtired."

"You sound like a protective father," Al teased.

"Uncle—a protective uncle." Terry grinned. He hated to see his friends leave, but he knew they were in safe hands. He knew he could trust God to lead them to someone who would continue where he'd left off.

The Friday-night sessions in the dormitory continued to grow, and Terry continued to search for new ways to live his beliefs without preaching. He arranged for a number of the men to participate in the Diabetes Foundation Walk/Run-a-Thon.

When he realized how much time he wasted riding the Honor Guard bus to and from assignments and how often someone would ask to borrow his reading material, he asked his mother to send him some religious tracts he could hand out to anyone requesting one. Before long, the men of his element depended on Terry to be carrying extra reading material each time they boarded the bus. In time he distributed as many as thirty-five tracts per trip.

But not everyone liked the JEEP who talked too much and who refused to drink with the guys. The men who believed themselves too tough for religion called him names: "Party pooper," "nerd," "wimp," "holy boy."

Taking on one person at a time, Terry chipped away at the enemy camp with his unrelenting cheerfulness. Terry made himself available at any time, night or day, to offer advice and encouragement to those needing advice or consolation.

However, Wes Conners, a self-proclaimed atheist, harassed him at every opportunity. The more people around to hear, the more Wes enjoyed humiliating Terry. He tried to smile and to laugh off Wes's jabs, but, pray as he might, it was a constant battle to maintain his cool toward the loud-mouthed braggart.

One hot, sultry morning, the entire unit had been assigned to attend a flag ceremony at the White House. As the men prepared for the full-uniform inspection, Wes spotted Terry carrying his Bible and another book and began his taunting. "So, holy boy, ya gonna flake today?" Terry smiled and turned away from the aggressor.

The sergeant in charge inspected each of the men's uniforms for lint or wrinkles or less than a mirror shine on the shoes. Then he reviewed the day's procedures. "The departure ceremony for Prime Minister Mulroney will be held on the back steps of the White House. It's stifling hot out there today, so be sure you're carrying your smelling salts—just a warning." Everyone understood the warning and checked under the rim of his hat to be certain his supply was intact.

Once the sergeant ordered the men to fall out, and they began boarding the bus, Wes began his irritating tirade again. "I see you brought along your magic book, Johnson. You know that your God is really nothing, a spook, a figment of your overactive imagination."

Terry opened his Bible as he waited to board the bus without giving Wes the satisfaction of an answer.

"Hey, Conners, knock it off," the guardsman standing behind Terry yelled. "Leave Johnson alone."

Wes snorted in derision. "Figures, a religious wimp like Johnson needs someone else to fight his battles."

The man in front of Wes turned and glared. "Cut it out, Conners. You're just spoiling for a fight."

Wes climbed on board and found a seat toward the back. "No threat where that pantywaist is concerned."

The three men between Wes and Terry boarded; then Terry climbed up the stairs and paused. He noticed where Wes sat and chose a seat as far from the troublemaker as possible. Standing near his chosen seat, Terry removed his jacket and hung it on the hanger, then sat down.

"Good choice, Johnson. Come back here, and you might have to stand up for something." Wes laughed at his own humor, while the guardsmen around him grumbled for him to stop the harassment.

"You're going to get him mad enough to fight you," one of Terry's friend's warned.

Wes broke into another round of hilarious laughter. "Ho, ho, right! Holy boy may fight me and get his halo bent!"

Anger rose inside Terry. He growled beneath his breath and stared out the window. The unbearably sticky mid-summer heat soared inside the loaded bus, setting everyone's nerves on edge. The bus's air conditioning couldn't begin to keep pace.

"Hey, holy boy—"

"Give it a break, Conners," one of the old-timers growled.

"Naw. Naw," Wes continued, "why don't you ask your God to give us some shade out there on the back steps today? As if He could!"

Terry glanced out the window at the passing scene. Getting angry won't solve anything, he told himself.

"Pack your clothes, holy boy, you're leaving today. You're gonna flake."

Terry clenched and unclenched his jaw. He could feel the muscles in his face tighten. His anger edging closer and closer to the boiling point, he stood up and turned to face his adversary. "Wes, that's enough."

"Oh, big threat!" Wes mimicked the voice of a frightened little girl.

Terry replied, his voice soft with warning, "Wes, you never know. You could flake, you know."

"Me?" Wes threw his head back and cackled. "I've been in the guard for a very long time! I've had many assignments worse than this! You'll fall out long before I will." He glanced around to be certain the other men were listening, then adjusted the cuffs on his shirt. "Why, even God Himself couldn't make me fall out."

A hush descended on the bus. One of the sergeants seated

in the front of the bus whirled about. "OK, Conners, you're pushing it too far. Cut it out."

Wes threw up his hands in innocence. "What can I say? I've been here too long. God can't make me fall out."

A chill ran up Terry's spine. He recalled the story of the priests of Baal defying God on Mount Carmel. He shot the man a look of sadness mixed with warning. "Wes, you shouldn't have said that."

The showoff threw his head back again and belly-laughed. When he'd finished his display of bravado, he noticed that the other men didn't seem to approve of his arrogance. In an effort to maintain the momentum of his attack, he added, "Like I'm really scared." The men eyed him with disdain, then turned away.

At the White House, Terry donned his uniform, located his assigned flag, the flag for the state of Wyoming, and took his place in line. The teasing among the five military units began almost immediately. Terry felt a jab in his back. "Good day for a flake, eh, flyboy?"

Terry grinned back at the smiling marine behind him. "Not on your life, jar head."

Chapter Twenty-six

Outside on the lawn in front of the White House portico, more than 400 people, the press, television crews, and presidential aides and staff waited in the hot sun for the pageantry to begin. A lectern stood in the center of the first landing, facing a tangle of cords and microphones of varying sizes, colors, and shapes.

When the sergeant in charge gave the signal, the Honor Guard representing the five divisions of the United States military marched onto the lawn carrying the state flags and forming a colorful backdrop for President Reagan and Prime Minister Mulroney. The oppressive heat bore down on the portico. Perspiration, combined with the itchy wool of his uniform, made Terry wish the officials would get on with it. Out of the corner of his eye, he caught a glimpse of Wes standing on the opposite side of the lectern. Terry shook his head at the man's audacious claims and steeled himself against the heat.

After what seemed like forever, President and Mrs. Reagan, along with Canada's prime minister and his wife, flanked by the customary entourage of Secret Service men, appeared at the portico's double doors. They smiled and posed for the cameras, then strode down a flight of steps to the podium. The President stepped up to the lectern and began his speech.

"Today is an auspicious occasion in the history of North America, when two countries, Canada and the United States, friends and brothers, have agreed to . . ."

Suddenly, out of the corner of his eye, Terry caught a movement from the other side of the President. Wes's flag wobbled, then fell with a loud crack, and Wes disappeared from view. Startled by the noise of the flag clattering down the steps, Reagan jumped and turned toward the sound. Immediately Secret Service agents whirled about and scanned the audience, searching for a possible assassin. Electrified by the sudden movement, members of the press aimed their minicams, and photojournalists set their cameras into action. The click of snapping cameras accompanied the clatter of the fallen flag's descent to the bottom of the marble staircase.

The flagman standing next to Wes reached into the band of his hat and removed the container of smelling salts. He knelt down and passed the vial under Wes's nose. Wes awakened to the ultimate humiliation. For a *coup de grâce,* he'd not only flaked, but he'd also wet his pants in front of more than 400 people on the steps of the White House.

The Wes Conners story went down in Honor Guard history as the worst flake ever recorded. From that time on, Wes never uttered a derisive word about Terry or his religion. Any who might have participated with Wes in harassing Terry denied their association with Wes. The next Friday night, attendance at the Bible study doubled.

At the end of the summer, Terry flew home to Portland on furlough. He was eager to spend time with his friends, but especially to talk with Elder Matula. The Bible teacher arranged to have Terry speak with his students. Terry told them about his days at their school and his nights out with the guys. He told them about the night he was supposed to have been with his friend, and the friend died in a car accident, driving while intoxicated. Most of them remembered Terry and the death of his friend. He told them of his military experiences and how God had guided him step by step.

Terry went back to his old neighborhood in northeast Portland. His mother and stepfather had long since moved to a small community outside the city limits, but Terry still felt a need to keep in touch with the old neighborhood. He talked with old friends, the ones he'd hung out with on the street corners after school. They told him about the L.A. gangs that had moved in and taken over. Terry asked about the friends missing from the group. As he recited their names, his friends who were present shook their heads. Out of the seven black children who had started first grade with him at Irvington Elementary School, all except Terry were either physically dead, mentally dead on heavy drugs, or in prison.

He drove back to his mother's home in Troutdale amid a blur of tears. "Why, Lord? Why me? Why did I alone escape?"

Back in Washington, D.C., the holiday momentum had already begun with autumn's changing colors. When he met again with his Friday-night group, they were making plans for their Christmas activities.

"You know, the city runs a 'Toys 4 Tots' program to collect toys for kids who won't get a regular Christmas. It would be fun to go to a large shopping mall and collect toys."

"Yeah, we could construct a gigantic wooden box, paint it up like a child's block or something, and then stand guard while people dropped toys in it."

A younger member of the group looked toward Terry. "Do you think the brass would let us go in uniform?"

Terry remembered the commander's words from the previous Christmas. "I think it can be arranged."

"Wow!" One guard, known for his roguish eye, whistled. "Think of all the chicks we can meet!"

"That's not why we're doing this," an old-timer reminded.

Terry thought for a moment. "You know, I think you've got something there. We could have a sign to tell the shoppers that we can speak only to those who contribute a toy."

Cries of "I like it!" and "It will work!" passed through the group. The men divided up the responsibilities, while Terry made the arrangements with the commander.

The second-year holiday volunteer program went better than the first. The Honor Guard's appearance at the shopping mall became an instant hit in the D.C. area, as did all the other charities in which they participated. Letters from community leaders flooded into Bolling headquarters, commending the guard for its spirit of service. The citizens of the city began to think of the Honor Guard as their own.

Purdee had been coming to Terry's Bible-study group for eight months, yet his attitude remained somewhat negative. One night he told Terry that he was attending a youth rap session at a local Baptist church. He said he liked the homelike atmosphere of the youth room. He asked Terry to join him.

"Sorry, man, but I can't tonight."

"Another time," Purdee waved and was gone. Later that evening, Terry had just finished showering when Purdee burst into his room. "Johnson, sit down. You're not going to believe what happened to me tonight!"

Terry obeyed while Purdee started his tale. "I was feeling really strange the moment I entered the youth room. I felt kind of dizzy, like I wasn't connecting or something. That's when it happened—I blacked out."

Purdee paced across the room, then back, to face his friend. "When I came to, it was like I was walking through a dark railroad tunnel toward the sunlight, and I was crying softly. The entire group were gathered around me, praying for me. I struggled to my feet and looked about the room.

"A coffee table lay shattered against the far wall. Lampshades were tilted at weird angles. The room looked as if a tornado had passed through. I asked what happened, and they said, 'Don't you remember?' "

"I looked at them blankly, since I didn't remember a thing. Then they said that when they'd begun to pray for me, I started talking crazy, saying things like, 'Religion is phoney.' I picked up a Bible and heaved it across the room." He paused and ran his hand across his closely cropped hair. "Then they said I threw the coffee table against the back wall. In spite of my destructive behavior, the people praying said that they felt a calmness come over the room and just kept praying."

Terry stared at Purdee, his face beaming with happiness and tears trickling down his cheeks. "Terry, remember Mac and his demon curses? He used some of his voodoo on me, and I didn't know it. But tonight, Jesus freed me."

The two men talked long into the night. Soon after, Purdee took formal Bible studies and was baptized into the Capitol Hill Church.

Chapter Twenty-seven

Purdee hung behind until other members of the Friday-night Bible-study group returned to their own rooms for bed. "There's someone who wants to talk with you."

Terry bent down and picked up a pamphlet one of the men had left on the floor of his room. "Sure, who is it?"

"John Banks. He's in the—"

At the mention of the name, Terry crumbled the pamphlet in his fist as anger coursed through him. "I know John Banks. What does he want with me?"

Purdee looked startled by the bitter tone in Terry's voice. "He and his wife are on the verge of splitting up. They want to talk with someone."

While Terry attempted to remove the wrinkles in the pamphlet he'd crushed, a battle raged within him. He remembered John Banks all too well. They'd met during T-flight training. And for some unknown reason, John despised Terry. The man had regularly gone out of his way to get Terry in trouble with his superiors. At first Terry tried to win him over with kindness, but the kinder Terry became, the nastier John treated him. Throughout T-training, Terry warred with himself to control his temper against John. And now, the man wants me to help him save his marriage? Terry thought. Talk about irony!

Terry's silence encouraged Purdee to continue the story. "I was lifting weights at the gym and got to talking with John. He said he was ready to leave his wife, Cathy, and just wished things could work out for them. I told him I knew someone

145

who could help them work things out." As he continued with his story, Purdee studied Terry's face for a reaction. "Well, John got all excited and said he'd love to meet this guy right away. Then he asked me your name."

Terry looked away from his friend. Purdee arched his eyebrow speculatively. "His reaction to your name was the same as yours was to his. Anyway, he did ask me to make arrangements for him and his wife to talk with you. He and his wife are Mormons, you know."

Terry's thoughts returned to Rick, an antagonist during basic training. He'd learned so much more about what he believed since then. Purdee waited for Terry's reply. When it wasn't forthcoming, he pressed the issue. "So? Can I tell him you'll help them? They have a six-month-old son."

Reluctantly, Terry agreed to see John and his wife.

The next evening Purdee and Terry went to John and Cathy's apartment. As Terry led the couple step by step through the basics of Christianity, the old antagonism sprang up over every issue discussed. Finally, in exasperation, Terry called the discussion to a halt. "Look, you know and I know that something isn't working here. Since you invited me here, consider my suggestion. For one week, let's give God's Word, the Bible, a chance." He hurried on before John could object. "Then if things don't change in one week, at least you can stand before God on the judgment day and honestly say you tried. And if it does work, we'll take it from there."

The first night they talked about the Mormon beliefs. The next night Terry explained how to become a Christian. Since Cathy had converted to Mormonism from Lutheranism when she married John, she had no trouble accepting what she heard. But John had been born and raised in his religion. At the end of the evening, Terry asked, "You have heard the story of Jesus. Would you like to accept Him into your lives?"

When Cathy answered Yes, a strange look came into John's eyes. "Something just happened to me that I can't explain." He ran his hand over his stubbled chin. "When you asked me to accept Christ, it . . . it was like . . . shackles fell from my mind. I feel . . . free. Yes, yes, yes, I want this Jesus living in me." A lump formed in Terry's throat as he watched his former adversary transform right before his eyes.

The Bankses attended the Capitol Hill Church the next Sabbath. After the services, Terry introduced them to the pastor and his wife, Elder and Mrs. Wintley Phipps.

A friendship developed between Terry and John as the couple studied God's Word with Terry. Before long, Cathy and John were baptized. Studying and praying together healed many of the rifts in their marriage, allowing them to build a relationship stronger and happier than they'd ever had in the past. When John's family learned of Cathy and John's conversion to Adventism, they tried to dissuade them. When all their efforts failed, John's family disowned him.

A few weeks after Cathy and John's baptism, John came to the dormitory to find Terry. "It's happened," John began, "a miracle. I'm being transferred to guard duty at the Pentagon."

"That's great, man. Congratulations." Terry shook his friend's hand. John had been hoping for months for the opportunity to join the Pentagon's security force.

"The only problem is, what will I do if the need arises, and I am expected to shoot to kill? I can't take another man's life—not now, since I gave my heart to the Lord. I honestly don't know what to do."

"I can only tell you what a wise colonel once told me. 'God needs Christian men in the military. Stick it out until He tells you to do otherwise.' In the meantime, pray that you will never have to go against your conscience."

Situated in the comfortable niche he'd carved out for himself during the last year and a half in the Honor Guard, Terry didn't realize how soon his advice to John would come back to confront him. A friend, René Rosa, told Terry that there were openings available at the Pentagon. Terry barely listened, since they only chose people with college experience for those posts. He didn't give it another thought until the day Sergeant Washington called him into his office. "Terry, remember when I told you I was putting in for a transfer? Well, it's come through."

"Oh, no, I'm going to miss you, man."

Sergeant Washington leaned forward in his desk chair and

exhaled. "That's not all, I'm afraid. They're bringing in a man especially to train the men for the bicentennial celebration of the signing of the Constitution. Sergeant Adams is a tough bird. He's already bragged about his plans to work you men seven days a week, with no exceptions."

Terry straightened and eyed his friend. "Oh—no Sabbaths off, right?"

The sergeant nodded. "You got it."

"Thanks for telling me ahead of time. I appreciate it."

"Do you know what you'll do?"

"Well, one thing is certain. I won't work on my Sabbath." Terry left the office in a daze. Maybe it's time to move on, he thought, or I could protest. I should go see the commander. If anyone can help me, he can.

When Terry told the Honor Guard commander his problem, the man shrugged. "Sergeant Adams is in charge of training. And if he says no exceptions, there's no way around it."

"Great," Terry mumbled as he left the commander's office. "I can just see myself now getting a dishonorable discharge for arguing with a sergeant!"

At supper, Terry told John and Purdee what had happened. "Why don't you apply to work at the Pentagon too?" John asked. "You do like to talk."

Purdee laughed. "Hey, I guess I'm lucky I'm in the rifle drill team, huh? So far, I haven't had any trouble."

Terry took his friend's advice and filled out an application, along with sixty other honor guardsmen. The night before the Pentagon appointments were announced, he prayed for God to direct in the decision.

The next morning, when he found his name on the list, he discovered a second surprise. He rushed to tell his friend, Sergeant Washington, about it. "Would you believe, my White House tour of duty ends on Friday, and Sergeant Adams is scheduled to arrive on Monday morning." Terry paused to catch his breath. "And René Rosa made it too. Isn't it incredible how God works out even the tiniest details?"

Sergeant Washington grinned at his eager young friend. "Only if we ask Him."

Chapter Twenty-eight

"While you will continue to live in the Honor Guard dormitory, you will no longer report to any Honor Guard functions. You will report directly to me, the head of the Public Affairs Office. And I report to the assistant secretary of defense." The marine corps major removed a stack of seventy-page books from his desk and handed one to each of the new tour guides. "Read this book. Memorize it. It contains the history of the Pentagon." The major hurried on. "For the next two weeks you will walk the halls of the Pentagon to familiarize yourself with the different military corridors, since you will be walking backward as you direct tours through the sensitive areas of the building complex. This is to prevent a guest from slipping away from the group." The major's steel-cold smile emphasized the importance of his words. "We don't want unauthorized individuals wandering at will through the complex now, do we? Oh, yes, the personnel here at the Pentagon will stay out of your way, not the other way around."

During his training to be a Pentagon tour guide, Terry discovered that the Pentagon selects men from the Honor Guard to fill two functions—tour guides, his department; and sentry duty, where his friend, John Banks, worked. A sentry stands beside the door to the office of the secretary of defense with a loaded .38 revolver. He is chosen for his marksmanship and appearance. All five branches of the military are represented in the Pentagon's staff of honor guardsmen.

The tour guides operate out of the Public Affairs Office. They are chosen for their personality and communication skills. President Carter founded the Pentagon tours in 1976 for the country's bicentennial celebrations. The tours were so popular with the tourists, the government decided to continue them. The guides conduct three different tours: one for the general public; another for high-school and political science students and other special groups; and a third for visiting presidents and honored dignitaries from other countries. At the end of each tour, the tour guide distributes comment cards that allow the visitors to evaluate the tour. The guide with the most cards returned with positive responses at the end of a month is deemed "Tour Guide of the Month."

The tours included the Hall of Heroes. These are the men who earned the Congressional Medal of Honor and other war-time medals. Terry always made a point of telling the visitors about Desmond Doss, the medic who saved so many lives during World War II. The next stop along the tour is at the Time/Life Corridor, where paintings and photographs taken during the battles of World War II are displayed. The next three corridors honor three branches of the military: the navy, the army, and the air force.

One corridor displays examples of all the official flags flown in the United States over the years. The Commander in Chief Corridor, Terry's favorite, has paintings of each president, with a larger painting of the current president along with paintings depicting the current president's involvement with the military during his administration.

Each tour guide must memorize the general history of each corridor, and he must choose one corridor as his specialty. Recalling information he had learned about the presidents from his American history teacher in high school, Mr. Thornsbury, Terry chose to specialize in the Commander in Chief Corridor. Terry immediately began collecting and including additional presidential trivia in his speech. He found the little-known facts of history fascinating. Once he developed his speech for the Commander in Chief Corridor, Terry set out to learn more about the other corridors. He visited with veterans of World War II to find additional bits of information about the war. Before long the other tour guides had nicknamed him "Mr. Trivia."

One morning, the assistant secretary of defense asked the major to arrange for one of the tour guides to take seventy political science majors from a local university through the Pentagon. The major chose Terry.

Terry introduced himself to the students and briefed them on Pentagon procedure. "We request that you stay with the group throughout the tour. If you have any questions, please feel free to ask them at any time." At first the students found it fascinating that he could walk backward and talk knowledgeably about the displays they were passing at the same time. Between corridors, when there was nothing of interest and nowhere for anyone to slip off to, Terry would turn and walk facing forward.

He had finished explaining about the history of the United States Coast Guard in the appropriate corridor and turned around to lead the group to the corridor honoring the Department of the United States Navy when he spotted Oliver North and his secretary, Fawn Hall, walking straight toward them. He knew they were probably heading for North's office in the annex across the street from the main Pentagon building. They'd recently appeared at the Iran-Contra hearings. Their faces were currently being splashed across every television newscast and newspaper in the country. Any political science major worthy of the title would recognize North and Hall in a minute.

Terry darted a glance first one direction, then the other, hoping to find a detour he could take in order to avoid direct contact. There was none. Terry decided his only way out was to bluff it. He thought that if he walked forward rather than backward, perhaps the students would assume there was nothing in the area worthy of note and miss recognizing the two celebrities. He stepped up the pace and continued walking and talking as North and his secretary passed. When Terry was certain they were out of sight, he turned around to continue his lecture. The corridor was empty. Seventy political science majors had vanished. Outrageous nightmares of seventy college students loose in the Pentagon caused him to shudder.

Frantic, he dashed down the hallway and around the corner. There, he found Oliver North and Fawn Hall backed up against a wall, with political science majors taking souvenir pictures and badgering them with questions. Terry stopped to regain his composure, then strode down the hall, mentally taking a quick tally of the group as he approached to be certain no one was missing.

"Let's keep it moving. That's enough now. You've detained Colonel North long enough." In his most brisk military manner, he herded them back down the corridor. This time he walked backward. As they turned the corner, Terry noted a smile of gratitude and relief on the colonel's face. The students gave him top marks on the comment cards at the end of the tour, but he wasn't so sure the colonel and his secretary would do the same. After a few weeks had passed, and he received no censure from his superiors, Terry could even see the humor in the situation.

Chapter Twenty-nine

"Don't you worry." Terry squeezed John Banks' elbow reassuringly. "Look how often God has come to my aid. He'll do the same for you. He promised." The possibility that he might one day have to use his revolver on another human being in the line of duty plagued John.

Terry and John's friendship had grown since John and Cathy's baptism. The two men spent whatever time they could together talking and praying. Terry loved hearing about the progress Cathy and John were experiencing spiritually and maritally. He also enjoyed hearing anecdotes about his godson, John, Jr.

"I overslept this morning and missed breakfast." Terry rubbed his growling stomach. "I'm going to run down to the cafeteria and get an orange or a sweet roll to tide me over until my lunch break."

As John opened the door, he glanced down at his watch. "I gotta run. I go on duty in just a few minutes." They split at the top of the stairs, John rushing toward Secretary of Defense Weinberger's office and Terry hurrying toward the cafeteria. At that moment, neither man knew the forces already set into motion that would vindicate his faith in God and His Word.

A young white man, disturbed over the United States' withdrawal of various trade restrictions on South Africa, decided to draw attention to the problem in his own way. He would assassinate Secretary of Defense Caspar Weinberger. For weeks, he cased the Pentagon. He familiarized himself with the building's floor plan until he knew it as well as any of the tour guides. By using the river entrance to the building, he'd timed how long it would take him to ride the escalator up to the second floor to the secretary of defense's office door. With any luck he could cover the ten feet to the defense secretary's office door, shoot the sentry guarding the door, and burst into Weinberger's office before the security guards down at the entrance had time to catch up with him. The man purchased a .45 automatic and the necessary ammunition. The young revolutionary knew he wouldn't come out of the attack alive, but, he reasoned, neither would Secretary of Defense Weinberger.

John had just assumed his post outside Weinberger's office when the protester strode up to the river entrance. Since the river entrance was only for Pentagon personnel, one of the two security guards asked for his ID. The man reached into his pocket as if going for his wallet, then, without warning, bolted full speed through the metal detector and across the foyer to the escalators. The metal detector sounded, and the guards shouted for him to stop or they'd shoot. He kept running. What caused him to leap onto the left moving staircase that went down instead of the right one going up, no one ever knew.

Determined, he'd almost reached the top of the staircase when he turned and pointed his gun at the security guards below, causing them to scatter for cover. One of the security guards managed to shoot him before he stepped off the escalator. The man tumbled down the stairs, landing at the feet of the man who shot him. On the second floor, less than ten feet away from where the man had been, John stood poised with revolver in hand, ready to shoot if necessary, to protect the secretary of defense.

Terry had just paid the cashier for his tray of food in the cafeteria when the first shot echoed through the hallway. He snapped alert. The shots had come from the direction of the secretary of defense's office a couple of corridors away.

"Oh, no. John's been shot!" Terry dropped the tray of food on the floor and charged down the hallway, passing other concerned people as if they were standing still. John still had his gun out by the time Terry reached him. Mass confusion was everywhere.

"Get back! Get back!" Terry shouted to the office workers hanging over the escalator stairs, trying to get a better view of the body. The guard below shouted up to Terry as he ran to the emergency phone to call the proper authorities. "Somebody shut the escalator off!" The second guard knelt beside the man and checked for vital signs. The security police sirens already filled the air when the guard stood up and shook his head slowly.

Terry walked over to where his friend stood trembling, his gun still in hand. A unit of the Pentagon police arrived and posted another guardsman at the secretary's door to allow John a twenty- to thirty-minute break to reestablish his equilibrium.

Terry stayed with him until John had to go back on duty. The facts leading up to the shooting untangled during the subsequent investigation. Life at the Pentagon quickly returned to normal. Only Terry and John could fully appreciate the extent of what happened that fateful morning. That evening, Terry went over to John and Cathy's home.

"How could the gunman have made such a stupid mistake as to jump onto the down escalator instead of the up?" John shook his head in amazement. "Christian or not, I would have had to shoot him. A few seconds' margin made all the difference."

Terry laughed. "Remember when I told you I couldn't hit the target to qualify and had to be held back, and how I later discovered why when my new roommate gave his heart to God? I guess our God deals in millimeters and fractions of seconds."

John gave his wife Cathy a hug. "And in the ability to tell one's left from one's right."

"I can relate to that," Terry chortled.

The next Sabbath morning, John told the story of God's answer to his prayer to the congregation at the Capitol Hill Church.

While John's days at the Pentagon might have been punctuated with excitement, Terry's never failed to be varied and interesting. The fact that he loved what he did became evident in each of his tours. And the tourists showed their appreciation for his enthusiasm by rating him high on their comment cards. The public relations office awarded him Tour Guide of the Month. The word spread. Various embassies told their visiting dignitaries when touring the Pentagon to request Mr. Trivia as their guide. When the chancellor of East Germany made his first visit to the United States, Terry was appointed to be his Pentagon guide.

While the East German chancellor and the secretary of defense talked over a special lunch in the executive dining room, the public relations official briefed Terry about the chancellor's tour.

"Give him a full thirty-minute tour. And whatever you do," Terry's superior cautioned, "don't upset him. This is his first visit to the United States."

Terry greeted the chancellor and his entourage at the secretary of defense's office door. By now he was undaunted by the important individuals he regularly toured through the building. He introduced himself and began the tour. His well-rehearsed speech never got in the way of answering their questions. They entered the Time-Life Corridor, and Terry pointed out the various photographs and paintings of World War II.

"Over here on your right," he explained, "is an actual photograph of the largest bombing mission over the German city of Berlin." Terry had learned so many interesting details about the photo from a local World War II veteran that he easily warmed to his subject. However, as he spoke he noticed strange looks sweeping over the faces of both the U.S. Secret Service men who had been assigned to protect the chancellor and over the faces of the chancellor's own security men. Not knowing what to make of it, he continued his presentation.

The chancellor studied the photograph for a few minutes in silence; then he pointed at one corner of the picture. "By the way, during the bombing you describe, my father was killed in that building right there."

Terry sucked in his breath. "Oh, I'm sorry," he mumbled feebly. The chancellor waved his hand and proceeded down the hallway.

Feeling terrible, Terry continued the tour in a much more subdued manner. Later, he was surprised when the chancellor sent an excellent letter of commendation to Terry for the tour he'd conducted. The department placed the letter in Terry's permanent file.

As his six months of special duty at the Pentagon came to an end, Terry knew nothing had changed back at the guard. The sergeant drilling the guardsmen for the upcoming bicentennial of the Constitution celebrations had done just what he promised, working the men seven days a week when necessary, allowing no exceptions. And he was still there.

Terry and his friends prayed together about his predicament during the week before his return to the White House assignment. Each morning at worship in the Honor Guard lounge, the morning worship group prayed for him.

The last morning of Terry's appointment at the Pentagon, the guardsmen met one last time before returning to their White House assignment. The public affairs officer called the meeting to order. "Gentlemen, your service here at the Pentagon during the last six months has been exceptional. Each one of you has done an excellent job representing the United States armed services and the Honor Guard. Secretary of Defense Caspar Weinberger has written letters of commendation for each of you, copies of which will be included in your permanent file." His assistant handed out the letters to the guardsmen as the officer spoke. "One more thing. I need to speak with the black guy with the big mouth."

"Johnson," someone called out. "That's gotta be Johnson." Even though there were a number of black guards, everyone agreed the public relations man could be speaking only about Terry.

The officer looked at Terry. "Airman Johnson, you need to report to the major's office immediately. You are all dismissed. Have a good day."

The same old feelings of inadequacy rumbled inside Terry

as he made his way to the marine major's office. Boy, I'm really in trouble this time, he thought. What could I have possibly done? As he walked, he went through every tour he'd conducted during the last few weeks step by step and could think of nothing that had happened to warrant censure.

He was conducted into the major's office. The major sat behind his desk staring down at the paperwork in front of him. Before Terry could act, the major barked, "Stand at attention in front of me."

"Oh," Terry groaned silently, "I am really gonna get burned this time." He remembered the tour with the East German chancellor. "Maybe, in spite of the letter of commendation he sent, the man reported my mistake to my superiors."

Finally, the major looked up at Terry. "According to our records, you have received four of the Tour Guide of the Month Awards handed out during the six months you've been here. Since this is highly unusual, unheard of, actually, the people of my office want to extend your service here at the Pentagon by a couple of months." Relief flooded Terry's face. The major smiled.

"Is that acceptable with you, Airman Johnson?"

"Oh, yes, sir!" Terry snapped off a smart salute.

Again, a slight smile broke at the corners of the marine major's mouth. "You're dismissed, Johnson."

When the other tour guides learned of Terry's extended appointment to the Pentagon, some credited it to Terry's incredibly good luck, others to his unbridled enthusiasm. But those who were close to him knew better.

Chapter Thirty

The festivities surrounding the bicentennial celebrations for the signing of the United States Constitution kept Terry's friends busy. While he was definitely grateful for the way the Lord had worked out the potential Sabbath problems, Terry had to admit that he felt pangs of envy as he watched them going off to first one gala celebration, then another. He didn't enjoy being on the outside of the action looking in. So when he learned that he'd been assigned to be one of the air force honor guardsmen who would guard the actual Constitution at the National Archives beginning September 13, he eagerly anticipated the event. His team would be responsible for twenty-four hours of the eighty-seven-hour vigil that would be held at the archives.

A guardsman from each of the military divisions, with the exception of the newest unit, the coast guard, would stand for the stretch of an hour at one of the four corners of the display case while thousands of American citizens and foreign visitors filed past.

"The public will be within close proximity to you men," the sergeant in command explained. "No matter what, you must stay in flight. There will be security guards nearby to ward off anyone who tries to accost you physically. If someone is harassing you, pray that a security guard will notice and come to your rescue, for you will have no other option but to stand there and take it." The sergeant continued. "Look snappy out there, guys. Dan Rather and a filming crew from CBS will be taping a segment for their evening newscast and will be using you men for backdrop." He finished explaining the procedures in detail. "I've posted the rotation schedule on the dormitory bulletin board. Read it. Memorize it, men. We want no screw-ups."

Terry felt the surge of adrenalin in the television crew's preshow frenzy. Camera crew, script persons, and gaffers alike rushed about the marbled foyer making last-minute checks before the scheduled taping. Terry wandered over to where Dan Rather sat at a small makeup table, glancing over his script while a makeup artist added the last dabs of color to his face and neck. As Terry drew closer, Mr. Rather looked up from his script and smiled. "How are you doing, airman?"

Terry grinned. "Fine, Mr. Rather. The other guardsmen and I have been looking forward to today's filming."

They talked for a few minutes on general topics. "It must be difficult to break into newscasting," Terry said.

The anchor studied Terry's face for a moment before answering. "National news—yes, I'd say it is. Are you thinking of going into TV journalism?"

Terry shrugged. "I've thought about it a time or two."

A man signaled from across the room. "Ready for you on camera, Mr. Rather."

The makeup person slipped the protective plastic apron from the star's neck as he stood up. "Airman, if you have a dream, just really go for it. If you apply the discipline you've gained in the military, you'll have no problem." The anchor hurried to his place before the cameras. Terry and the other guardsmen took their places at the Constitution display.

Once the television crew left, the guardsmen resumed the hour-by-hour rotation schedule. The air force honor guardsmen stood at the top left-hand corner of the document. A long line of people passed by. Some stopped to read portions of the historical document; others, as predicted, tried to make the four guardsmen on duty smile or laugh.

After the twenty-four-hour rotation at the National Archives, Terry returned to his regular responsibilities as tour guide at the Pentagon. Terry pinned on his tour guide badge, checked his neck scarf, and headed down the hall to the

visitors' lounge, where a group of senior citizens waited—the
first tour of the morning. Having received advice from friends,
the group specifically requested Mr. Trivia as their guide.

He greeted the fifty to sixty members of his tour enthusiastically. After his brief introduction, he began the tour. As
usual, the tourists were fascinated with his confident presentation delivered while walking backward. In each corridor, the
group had dozens of questions for him, which he answered
with humor and wit. They found the Time/Life Corridor fascinating, since they'd all lived through World War II. They'd
entered the army section of the building when Terry cast a
glance over his shoulder and noticed that the army chief of
staff office doors were open.

Terry put his finger up to his lips. "Be very quiet as we pass
the United States Army chief of staff's office. The general is
working inside." Unaware of the military man walking down
the hall behind him and carrying a fresh cup of coffee, Terry
waved his free hand toward the open doors and into the arm
of the four-star general just as he was about to take a quick
sip of the steaming liquid.

Terry whirled about in time to see hot coffee splash down
the front of the startled general. The senior citizens gasped in
horror, but they felt nothing like the terror Terry was feeling.

Terry grabbed a handkerchief from the hand of one of the
quick-thinking tourists. "Here, let me help you."

The officer stared down at his coffee-stained shirt. "No, no!
That's all right, airman." The general looked up and noted the
fright on Terry's face and laughed. "I guess you were so worried about being quiet for the chief of staff that you ran into
the chief of staff. Don't worry, I have another shirt in my
office." He laughed again and walked into his office.

Still shaken, Terry completed the tour and bade the visitors
goodbye. Once they left, he headed for the Honor Guard
lounge and stretched out on one of the cots. While he knew
that technically the officer was at fault for not watching out
for a tour guide, he also knew that the four stars on the man's
shoulder could supersede guilt or innocence.

He'd rested only a few minutes when he had to go out on

his second tour. He did his best to build enthusiasm as he took the large group of tourists through the halls. Somehow he got through the day. As Terry prepared to leave, his superior handed him a note from the office of the chief of staff for the United States Army. The note commended Terry for his exceptional conduct as a Pentagon tour guide. The general never mentioned one word about the morning encounter or the spilled coffee.

More and more visitors requested to be in Mr. Trivia's tour group. More awards and commendations were placed in his permanent file. At the end of the extension, he was asked to stay on at the Pentagon for a while longer. No tour guide had ever had his appointment extended once, let alone a second time. Terry didn't understand it, but he praised God for it, since the hard-nosed Sergeant Adams was still in charge of running the White House Honor Guard.

The first of January in 1988, Terry learned he was to return to the White House. He saw two rotations of guardsmen leave the Pentagon to return to the regular Honor Guard unit. Each had been given a "hate to see you go" letter of commendation for his service from the secretary of defense. He expected to receive the same courtesy. At morning assembly, the major in the Public Affairs Office told him that they had requested for him to stay longer, but the commander of the Honor Guard had refused. The major made no mention of the customary letter. Disappointed, Terry returned to Bolling Air Force Base without even a simple thank-you note.

Terry hated the feeling that somehow he was slinking away into oblivion. Doesn't anybody care enough to say goodbye? he thought. The major could at least have shaken my hand and wished me well. Depressed, he arrived back at the dormitory in time for his first Honor Guard "commander's call" in over a year. He joined the rest of the men in the assembly room. The elements grouped themselves together in various sections of the room. Terry joined the second element, over on the right, by the large plate-glass windows that looked out onto the dormitory parking area. As he looked about the room, he shook his head upon seeing so many new faces. He felt he'd never get used to the military's constant change of personnel.

The sergeant shouted, "Atten-hut!" When the commander and the Honor Guard flag bearer entered the room, a series of loud cracks resounded throughout the room as the men of the different elements clicked their heels together, each element trying to click the taps on the inside of their shoes the loudest.

"At ease."

The men sat down. Terry glanced out the window at the snowbanks surrounding the parking lot in time to see a familiar Pentagon staff car drive into the lot and park. A man dressed in civilian clothes got out of the car. Seconds later, the stranger entered the assembly room and handed the Honor Guard commander a small box and a note.

The commander looked down at the note, then stepped up to the lectern. "Normally we read the letters of commendation from the secretary of defense for the men returning to us from Pentagon duty. But today, I have the honor of presenting a Joint Service Medal to one of our guardsmen to wear on his uniform for the rest of his military career."

The men burst into applause. The commander waved them silent. "Airman Terry Johnson, will you come forward, please?"

Terry stumbled forward to a second round of applause. The commander pinned the medal on Terry's uniform, then shook the speechless airman's hand. He had trouble concentrating until the commander came to the last announcement on his list. "As most of you know, Sergeant Adams left last Friday for his new assignment. So, now, I'd like to introduce you to your new sergeant, Sergeant Purcell."

While the new sergeant spoke a few words to his men, Terry searched the crowd and caught Purdee's attention. Purdee grinned and gave him a thumbs-up sign. God had worked everything out for him once again. He had left for the Pentagon assignment on Friday; Sergeant Adams took over the element on Monday. He had returned on Monday to learn that Sergeant Adams had transferred from the element the Friday before. Terry shook his head in amazement. Talk about an eye for detail!

The White House
Washington, D.C.
January 1988–February 1989

Chapter Thirty-one

One night, soon after returning to Bolling Air Force Base from a two-week leave, Terry stared down at the anemic total left in his savings account. His new car was draining his finances quickly, yet for days he had been impressed to give up his part-time job to spend all of his spare time giving Bible studies. He had more interests than he did spare hours. But the emaciated savings account argued strongly against making such a move.

Maybe the time isn't right, he thought. But when will the right time arrive? "God," he prayed over his savings account booklet, "You know I need the extra money . . ."

Familiar words popped into his mind. "Don't worry. I will take care of you."

Terry fell to his knees. "All right, Lord. You've done a good job so far taking care of me. It's all Yours." The next morning he quit the extra job.

His cash flow didn't improve during the next few days. As he opened his wallet, he shook his head. I'll just have to go to the bank tomorrow morning and withdraw more money from my savings account, he thought.

Having no assignment that morning, he drove to the bank branch closest to the base and parked his car. Hurrying into the bank, he filled out a withdrawal slip and stepped up to the first available teller. The teller, a young woman with short brown hair and tired brown eyes, smiled.

"May I help you?"

"I'd like to withdraw sixty dollars from my savings account. Two twenties and two tens, please." Terry handed her his savings book and the withdrawal slip.

She flashed him a professional smile. "Right away, sir." While she processed his withdrawal and removed the cash from the drawer, the woman glanced up at Terry. "Looks like it might turn out to be a nice day."

Handing the cash envelope and his savings book back to him, she smiled once more.

"Thank you very much, Mr. Johnson. Have a nice day."

"Thank you," he called, rushing from the bank to his car. Terry unlocked the car door and hopped in. He inserted the key in the ignition and fastened his seat belt before he remembered the cash in the envelope. He thought he'd better put the cash in his wallet before he lost it. Undoing the seat belt, he reached into his back pocket and removed his wallet. Mumbling to himself about being late for lunch, he counted out the money—20, 40, 50, 60. He stopped and stared—two twenties and two tens equaled $60.00. Then why were there more bills still in the envelope? He counted the rest of the cash—20, 40, 50, 60. A hundred and twenty dollars? How could the teller have made such a mistake? She must have counted out the cash twice by accident, he reasoned.

A smile broke over his face as he started the engine and backed out of the parking space. "Thanks, Lord. Somehow, You always manage to come through for me, don't You? What a blessing!"

He switched on the radio, leaned back, and whistled to the music as he drove back to base. This is definitely my lucky day, he mused.

Terry didn't think about the extra sixty dollars in his wallet until bedtime. Then, as he placed his wallet and car keys in his locker, he suddenly remembered. A tiny gnat of guilt buzzed somewhere at the back of his mind. He picked up his Bible to have his evening worship, and the gnat of guilt grew larger, into a persistent wasp. He brushed it aside and settled down for the night but couldn't shake the thought of that unearned money in his wallet.

Voices disturbed his sleep, voices that said, "Terry, it's not your money. You've got to give it back."

Preferring to believe that the voice was the devil trying to discount the miracle God had performed, he buried the thoughts beneath more pleasant ones, only to have them resurface.

All night long, he battled his conscience. The first thing in the morning, he headed for the bank. As the security guard opened the doors for the new day of business, Terry rushed into the bank and glanced about. The teller he'd dealt with the day before was nowhere in sight. He spotted an older woman with frizzy gray hair and wire-rimmed glasses hunched over a cluttered desk. He hurried over to her.

"Ma'am, I need your help. Yesterday there was a teller working line five." He described the teller's height and appearance. "I need to talk with her. Do you know where she is?"

The gray-haired woman glanced toward one of the office doors, then back at Terry. She gave him a disdainful smile. "Oh, you mean Mrs. Taylor. I'm sorry, but she's in counseling right now."

Terry frowned. "What about?"

The woman bristled at his harsh tone. "I beg your—"

Terry pounded his fist in the palm of his hand. "I need to see your bank manager right away."

"I'm sorry, sir." The woman rose from her desk to face the insistent young man. "That won't be possible, for, you see, he's the one counseling Mrs. Taylor."

"I'm sorry to be so insistent, but I need to see him right now!" Without another word, he strode over to the closed door marked Manager.

The bank employee rushed after him. "Wait! I'll tell him someone is here to see him."

Terry agreed. The woman opened the office door and closed it behind her.

Seconds later, the bank manager stepped out of his office

and gave Terry a grave look of irritation. Terry peered over the bank manager's shoulder at an ashen-faced woman sitting in his office. He recognized her right away.

"I really am quite busy right now, young man. If you will make an appointment with my assistant—"

Terry jutted his chin forward and thrust the cash envelope into the startled man's hands. "Sir, this will only take a moment of your time. I believe this sixty dollars is yours." Terry started to explain what had happened the day before when the teller in the office burst into tears. The sobbing woman leaped from the chair and rushed into the bewildered young man's arms.

"Do you know what you just did? You saved me my job." Her voice came in short gasps. "If you had been ten minutes later, I would have been fired. Thank you, thank you, thank you, for being such an honest man."

Terry patted her shoulder awkwardly. "Well, I-uh, I'm glad I could help."

The bank's employees gathered around as the bank manager explained what had happened. "You see, Mrs. Taylor has worked for us for only four weeks, and this was the second time she came up short of cash at the end of the day. We thought she'd stolen the money and were ready to let her go."

"I didn't know what I would do if I lost this job," Mrs. Taylor sobbed. "I needed this job desperately to support my year-old daughter, Casey. My husband walked out on me three months ago."

As he left the bank, Terry couldn't believe how close he'd come to wrecking this woman's future and that of her child. He whistled to the snappy tune blaring from his radio as he drove back toward the base. His wallet felt slimmer, but his soul bulged with happiness.

Chapter Thirty-two

After parking his car in the dormitory parking lot, Terry jogged over to the mess hall. He burst through the door just as the kitchen staff prepared to close the serving lines. "So how ya doin'?" he asked the airman who was about to turn the lock on the serving area door. "Think I can get a few scraps of leftover food?"

The man shrugged. "Sure, why not. Help yourself." Filling his plate with food, Terry headed toward a group of friends still lingering at one of the tables.

"Where ya been, Johnson? You almost went without."

"I know. I had to make a quick trip into Georgetown this morning." Terry thought about relating what had happened at the bank, then reconsidered. These guys won't be impressed, he thought. They'll think I'm stupid for being honest. He smiled to himself. He felt great. If this is how stupid feels, he thought, I'll take it over smart any day. He jabbed his fork into a tomato wedge and looked up. "So, what's happening here?"

One of the guardsmen looked up from the slice of apple pie he was finishing. "Nothing much, outside of the congressional dinner we're on for tonight."

Terry attacked a lettuce leaf with his fork and stuffed it into his mouth. "Am I scheduled? I forgot to check the bulletin board this morning."

"I don't think so, but you'd better check," the friend advised.

After finishing his meal, Terry checked the list. His name

wasn't there. Since he had time on his hands, he went for a short walk. By the time he returned to the dormitory, Terry had decided he was right to quit his part-time job in order to expand the number of Bible studies he could give. He would trust God to take care of the financial side of it.

Three days later, the Honor Guard commander called Terry into his office. "Johnson, I received two letters in the mail this morning. One from a Mrs. Lynn Taylor and the other from the local bank president. I thought you'd like to hear them." The commander read the letters telling about the returned $60.00 and how impressed they were with Terry's honesty. "You have done the Honor Guard proud, son. I've decided to place these letters in your permanent file."

Terry beamed with pride. "Thank you, sir."

At the next commander's call, the commander told the story of Terry's honesty to the entire unit, then called him forward. "I have chosen to present you a step promotion to senior airman for your exemplary behavior as a member of the Honor Guard." All of the men knew a step promotion is the only air force promotion that doesn't require testing and that is seldom awarded during peacetime. The promotion also made it possible for Terry to attend NCO (Noncommissioned Officer) preparatory school, which would advance him to the rank of sergeant.

"I-I don't know what to say, sir." As the commander shook Terry's hand, Terry suddenly remembered that a pay raise accompanied such an appointment. He bit his lip when he realized how God had blessed his honesty. When he received his first paycheck after the promotion, his paycheck was increased, almost to the penny, the amount he would have made if he'd kept the part-time job. And his classes for NCO Prep began the following week.

At 7:55 on Monday morning, Terry and thirty other airmen reported to the training center for classes. The instructor, Sergeant Casillo, introduced himself.

"You are no longer a part of your unit on base. You are assigned to me for the next three weeks. Each day from 8:00 a.m. to 5:00 p.m. your classes will include seminars on leadership, counseling, and managing people." The sergeant scanned the circle. "Since we will be spending a lot of time together during the next few weeks, I would like to know each of your future plans and goals." One by one, the men in the circle stood and told what they wanted to do with their lives after leaving the military.

When Terry's turn arrived, he said, "My name is Terry Johnson. I plan to study to become a minister."

Sergeant Casillo smiled. "What denomination?"

"Seventh-day Adventist."

A strange look crossed the sergeant's face. "Interesting. I'd like to speak with you for a few minutes after class." Then he moved on to the airman sitting beside Terry.

Terry waited after class until the last of his classmates had left before approaching the sergeant. "You wanted to see me, sir?"

"Yes. I was interested in learning a bit more about Seventh-day Adventism. You see, my grandmother is a Seventh-day Adventist. She used to take me to church with her whenever I visited her home in New Jersey."

"Really? What church did you attend?"

An instant friendship developed between the two men. Sergeant Casillo admitted to having a bad smoking problem. "I seem to remember that your church has a plan to help stop smoking, doesn't it?" Terry promised to get some pamphlets from the local Adventist Book Center to help the sergeant break his habit.

Sergeant Casillo's training seminars included lectures by visiting air force officers. These lectures usually occurred just before lunch. Since the program ran on a tight schedule, if the guest speaker spoke for too long, the airmen would not have enough time to get through line and eat before their afternoon classes began.

One morning, an air force colonel who had the reputation of being a tough, heartless officer made a presentation to the group. He was to speak on how he advanced from being an enlisted person to a commissioned officer during the Vietnam War. The man waxed eloquent and long-winded as he told his war stories.

The airmen glanced at the clock on the wall, then at Sergeant Casillo. Being only a sergeant, Casillo wasn't in a position to tell a colonel to sit down. There was nothing to do but smile and hope the colonel would wind down soon.

The man talked well into the lunch hour and showed no sign of stopping. With only fifteen minutes left to eat, Terry sighed. It would be a long afternoon if they all missed lunch. Something had to be done, but what? Well, if no one else will do something . . . Terry could feel his stomach tighten and his palms break out in a sweat as he considered his options. Finally he raised his hand.

The colonel nodded toward Terry. "Do you have a question?"

Terry stood up and gave the colonel his most winning tour guide smile. "Colonel, I'd like to thank you for the excellent job you've done this morning. You've inspired each one of us. And we all hope we can come to you with questions in the future."

The class members broke into enthusiastic applause.

Daunted by the unusual turn of events, the colonel glanced at Sergeant Casillo, who only shrugged; then he looked around the circle of applauding airmen. "Well, I guess that's my cue to go."

After Sergeant Casillo thanked the colonel for his presentation, the colonel left the room. The door closed behind the colonel. A couple of the airmen dashed to the window and watched to be certain the colonel went straight to his car. "He's in his car," they hissed simultaneously.

Pandemonium broke out as the class members threw their hats into the air and cheered Terry. Sergeant Casillo laughed so hard, tears streamed down his face. "It couldn't have been better if I'd planned it."

Toward the end of the three weeks of classes, Sergeant Casillo announced that three awards would be presented at the graduation exercises: the Academic Excellence Award, the Air Force Excellency Award, and the Speech Award.

Sergeant Casillo explained the significance of each award to them. "The Academic Excellence Award will go to the airman who scores the highest number of points on the final examination. You as a class will nominate the person whom you believe to be the most positive and encouraging member of the class for the Air Force Excellency Award. This individual will receive a personally engraved plaque as well as have his name engraved on the wall plaque here in the training center." The sergeant continued. "Before completing the course, each of you will be required to give a speech in front of the class. This is to prepare you, as sergeants, to give briefings in front of unit commanders. The top five speakers will give the same speeches in front of a second panel of judges," he explained. "And the top one chosen will receive the Speech Award at graduation."

Terry badly wanted to win the third award. While he knew he had no control over a popularity vote for the excellency award, and he doubted his grades would be high enough to earn him the academic award, he felt he at least had a chance when it came to public speaking. Remembering a book he'd read while in high school called *The Power of Positive Thinking*, by Norman Vincent Peale, Terry chose as his subject "You Can't Fail Unless You Want To."

He spent the next week writing and practicing his speech. Due to the seminar speeches he'd given while in high school, Terry felt comfortable when he got up to speak before his classmates.

The next morning, Sergeant Casillo announced the top five speakers chosen. Terry's name was on the list. "You five will present your speeches before a panel of officers. The name of the speaker chosen to receive the award will be announced at the graduation exercises."

Chapter Thirty-three

The thirty-one graduates of the NCO training program listened attentively as the guest speaker, a general from the Pentagon, presented the graduation address. As the applause following the speech died, Sergeant Casillo stepped up to the lectern. "It is now my pleasure to announce the award winners from today's graduating class. The Award for Academic Excellence, or the John Levinto Award, as it has been named to honor the latest person to receive the Medal of Honor, goes to Sonya Becker." Senior Airman Becker walked to the lectern and claimed her award to the applause of her classmates.

After the photographers finished shooting pictures of Senior Airman Becker receiving her award from Sergeant Casillo, and she had returned to her seat, the sergeant announced the second award. "You as a class voted for the recipient of the Award of Excellence." He went on to detail the significance of the award. "The name of the winner of the Award of Excellence will be inscribed on the official plaque in the NCO preparatory office. He will also receive this personal plaque to take with him.

"To the airman you as a class consider the most positive and most encouraging member of the group. Terry Johnson, will you come forward, please?"

The class applauded as Terry walked to the dais. The two friends posed for the official photographer; then Sergeant Casillo nodded for Terry to go back to his seat. He had just sat down when the sergeant announced, "Today is a first. This has never happened before; I've never known a graduate to receive two of the three awards." Sergeant Casillo cleared his throat, then continued, "Terry, come on up here one more time so that I may present you with the plaque and the letter of commendation from the panel of judges for the Speech Award."

Embarrassed, Terry made his way to the front, accompanied by his friends' thunderous applause. Sergeant Casillo raised his hands to silence the clapping. "Not only did Terry earn perfect scores from each of the judges for his presentation, but he so impressed them that they are doing something that has never happened before. They are inviting him to return as the guest speaker for the next NCO graduation."

While Sergeant Casillo spoke, Terry looked at the plaque in his hand. How far he'd come since the frightened second-grader struggled to make himself understood before an angry teacher! Did he feel lucky? No. Proud? No. He felt incredibly humbled. He knew that any credit for this victory belonged to his loving family and to the Christian teachers who cared enough to make a difference in his life.

Sergeant Casillo called him aside after the graduation service, "You know, I've accepted a promotion, so I'll be leaving Bolling, but I want to finish our Bible studies."

"Oh, well, I could give you a complete set of lessons, and you could take them with you. By the way, where are you going?"

"They've asked me to head up an NCO training program at a base in Hawaii."

Terry shook his head and grinned. "Rough assignment there."

Sergeant Casillo shrugged and smiled. "Well, what can I say? You know, you should apply for the position of NCO training assistant. You're a natural."

They walked to the door of the auditorium. Terry looked at his friend. They'd become good friends in such a short time. "You will keep in touch, won't you?"

Sergeant Casillo gave him a friendly punch on the arm. "You bet, Sergeant Johnson."

The added stripes on Terry's sleeve completely changed his status when he returned to funeral detail. The younger, newer guys he'd never met before were tripping over themselves to please him. "Yes, sir. May I help you, sir?"

Having gained recognition for his ability to speak well in public, Terry was chosen to act as narrator for a number of official ceremonies, including the placing of the United States Air Force wreath at the Tomb of the Unknown Soldier by the visiting president of West Germany.

He also began receiving invitations from all over the base to speak. A number of air force officials requested copies of his speeches. As more and more people heard him speak, a new opportunity for witnessing opened. Terry had wanted to conduct Revelation seminars on base for some time. But he needed a large-enough space and some audiovisual equipment. The logical place to hold the meetings would be the base chapel. However, he'd never heard of anyone being allowed to conduct religious meetings other than the scheduled church services.

When he entered the chapel coordinator's office, the sergeant in charge looked up from her desk and smiled. "You're Terry Johnson, aren't you? Won't you sit down?"

"Yes, ma'am." He sat in the chair indicated.

She folded her hands on the desktop in front of her. "So, Sergeant Johnson, what can I do for you?"

"I'm trying to get a study of Revelation going on Wednesday night. I know it's hard in the military, since you can't teach anything to offend another's religion, but—"

Before he could finish explaining, she waved away his concerns. "Don't even worry about it. What size classroom do you need?" She reached in her desk and took out a consent form for the use of the chapel.

She's probably thinking this is a one-night program, Terry thought.

She shoved the paper and a pen in front of him before he could answer. "Here, sign this paper, and it's yours every Wednesday night until you leave Bolling."

Terry couldn't believe his fortune. No one had ever been

granted carte blanche before. On the way back to his dormitory, he thought about the way God opens doors.

Months earlier, Terry had gotten excited over a book he'd read on living by faith by George Mueller. After reading it, he decided to save five dollars out of each paycheck in order to buy the supplies he'd need for conducting the meetings. As his savings grew, letters containing totally unsolicited money for his ministry arrived regularly.

Terry rushed to his locker and removed his secret stash of cash hidden in the rim of a hat—$637.00, two dollars more than the amount he needed in order to buy the materials for the seminar.

Being a sergeant, Terry had to be even more circumspect than previously when inviting people, as his invitation could be misinterpreted as an order. The first night of the Revelation seminar, seven men showed up at the base chapel, including Eric Hayes, a brash and aggressive ex-Catholic from California. Eric was an exception to Terry's usually silent approach to outreach. They'd met in the base lunchroom after Eric had been in the guard less than three months. Terry felt impressed to invite the JEEP to the Wednesday-night meetings.

After the first meeting, Eric challenged Terry. "You know, Sergeant Johnson, I don't agree with all that you said tonight."

Terry packed the leftover forms from the evening's lesson into his briefcase. "Let's sit down and talk about the issues that are bothering you."

Eric's quick mind probed into the truths presented. His piercing blue eyes bored into Terry as he demanded proof for everything presented that evening.

"Look, Eric, don't take my word for it. It's not me making these claims; it's your own Bible speaking. Look it up for yourself."

Week after week, Eric attended the seminar meetings and fought against the issues presented. When Terry presented the topic of life after death, Eric exploded. "I have never heard anything so ridiculous in my life. Everyone knows that after death, a soul goes to purgatory before earning the right to go to heaven."

By this time, Terry knew that no amount of argument would sway his friend. "Look, I don't know anything about your purgatory, but I'll tell you what. If you can convince me from the Word of God that purgatory does indeed exist, I'll believe it. While you're accumulating texts to prove your point, look over my list of texts that substantiate what I said tonight."

Two nights later, the last of the Friday-night Bible-study group had left Terry's room when Eric burst through the door. Eric's blue eyes glinted with sincerity. "Terry! You're right."

"Hi, Eric." Terry yawned and stretched. "I'm right about what?"

"Purgatory, hell, the grave, everything. It's all in the Bible. It's so clear I don't know how I could have missed it. I honestly have never read such things before."

"I know what you mean. There's so much in God's Word to learn, I feel like I've only scratched the surface." Terry picked up his Bible and opened it reverently. "One of my high-school teachers says that no matter how often he reads a particular text, he continues to uncover additional truths."

Eric frowned. "Can we ever have all the answers?"

Terry shrugged. "Yes and no. I think we'll have all the answers necessary in order to be ready for Jesus' coming, but I imagine even eternity won't be enough time to reveal everything there is to know about God."

Eric searched Terry's face. "Would you help me learn more about God, I mean away from the meetings, one to one?"

Would he! Terry had to swallow the joy bubbling up inside him. "Sure, I'd love to. What time's best for you?"

Chapter Thirty-four

Terry picked up his dummy rifle and took his place in line for the weapons cordon. The Honor Guard would be part of Secretary of Defense Caspar Weinberger's retirement ceremony. The sergeant in charge of the ceremony reviewed the procedure. "President Reagan's helicopter will land at the Pentagon. He will disembark and walk through the Honor Guard cordon. I don't need to tell you that representatives of the press from all over the world will be in attendance."

Cameras snapped, purred, and flashed as the members of the Honor Guard marched out onto the field in preparation for the arrival of the President's helicopter. It was late. Reporters and official dignitaries milled about the area impatiently as the guardsmen remained at attention.

Terry stared straight ahead, blocking out the world around him, until a tiny spider landed on his left cheek. The insect's legs tickled. Terry flexed a muscle in his cheek in an attempt to dislodge the uninvited guest. The spider obliged Terry by pattering across the bridge of his nose, onto the guardsman's right cheek, and up to the rim of his hat.

Terry took a deep breath of relief. It was common for insects to land on the men while they stood in flight, especially bees. For that reason, experienced guardsmen knew never to wear cologne. With the irritant gone, Terry resumed his mindless state until a tiny dot lowered itself on a slender thread from the rim of Terry's hat, right down the middle of his forehead, stopping just short of touching Terry's upper lip.

178

Terry extended his lower lip and gently blew at the yo-yoing spider. As if beckoned by her tiny comrade, a honeybee landed on Terry's right ear. While the bee didn't sting, the buzz and the vibration it caused tickled unmercifully. The bee must have liked what she found, for within seconds of her landing, one of her sisters came in for a landing on Terry's other ear and started humming her favorite tune. Terry had visions of the two bees parading into his ear canals and either meeting in the middle somewhere or attacking the walls of his inner ear when they discovered they couldn't turn around. Instead, the bees continued their own ritualistic dance on his ear lobes.

Frozen by protocol, Terry watched the spider scale his upper lip and rappel to the tip of his nose. The three creatures remained on their platforms for the arrival of the President of the United States and throughout the entire ceremony honoring the former secretary of defense. And no breathy attempts by Terry could convince any of the three to leave their choice front-row seats.

Pictures of Washington, D.C.'s, homeless flashed across the television screen during the late-night network news. "What would happen," Terry mused to Eric, "if every Christian in the entire world contributed ten dollars to the problem of the homeless? It would certainly go a long way toward alleviating the situation." By this time Eric had begun attending the Capitol Hill Church each Sabbath with Terry.

As Eric rose to his feet, he snorted. "I can't see that ever happening."

"Maybe not," Terry interrupted. "But that shouldn't stop us."

Eric eyed Terry suspiciously. "What are you suggesting?"

"Just that. What would happen if we both took ten dollars from each paycheck to use for helping other people?"

Eric sat back down. "You're serious, aren't you? Where would we start?"

"I don't know—"

Eric thought for a few seconds. "Food, that's what the homeless need most, food."

"Yeah, we can't start a soup kitchen or anything, but we

could make up bag lunches and hand them out."

"I like that! How much can a sandwich, an apple, and a few cookies cost, anyway?"

"We could always stick in a tract for them to read while they ate the lunch."

Eric jabbed his friend. "You and your tracts!"

"Don't knock it—it works."

With their first $20.00, they bought a large container of peanut butter, a loaf of whole-wheat bread, and a jar of grape jelly, along with a supply of cookies, fruit, and lunch sacks. They assembled the lunches, then drove into the capital city. Once they reached the inner city, it didn't take them long to spot potential customers. They enjoyed the experience so much, Eric and Terry decided to hand out lunches every Friday afternoon.

News of Terry and Eric's activities spread through the dormitory. Others asked to join. Rather than allow the group to grow too big and impersonal, Terry divided the volunteers into groups of five to ten men each.

On Sabbaths, Terry, Eric, and Purdee would attend church together at the Capitol Hill Church. Terry could see both men growing spiritually almost daily. He praised God for the changes happening within himself. One Sabbath, after a particularly inspiring sermon, Eric whispered to Terry as they were leaving the church, "You know, I wish more whites would become Seventh-day Adventists."

Terry laughed out loud. "Oh, I'm sorry, Eric. I guess I never considered the fact you've only attended the Capitol Hill Church with me. There are plenty of white SDAs, I assure you. Next Sabbath I'll take you to a predominantly white church, OK?"

They attended the Sligo Church. The church members went out of their way to welcome the three men. After the service, they invited the guardsmen to a potluck. All the way back to base, Eric marveled about the church service and the people's friendliness. While Eric had enjoyed Capitol Hill's black worship service, he responded enthusiastically to the more liturgical service he'd experienced at the Sligo Church. The discovery that Seventh-day Adventism is indeed a worldwide organization spurred his interest.

The short-term appointments to the Honor Guard kept people coming and going all the time. The decision to leave not only the Guard but also the military was one of constant discussion, especially for the men who'd decided to give their lives over to Christ. They would get together and discuss their plans.

"What does He want me to do? Surely God expects more from me than I can give Him while in the military," Eric suggested one night.

Terry didn't like the thought of men using their religion as an excuse for leaving the military early. He used the text in Colossians about servants being loyal to their masters as his argument. "Besides, look at me. I've done a whole lot more in the service than I could ever have done out."

Eric thought about Terry's advice, then came up with a plan of his own. "Maybe I can take classes at Columbia Union College while I'm still in the military. That way the air force will cover 75 percent of the expenses, and I can still complete my obligations to the Honor Guard."

However, Kevin, one of Terry's roommates, held a different conviction regarding his future. Since he'd not known of Adventism when he joined, he felt God had other plans for him now that he'd given his heart to Christ. Kevin had joined the Honor Guard at nineteen and at first made fun of Terry and his religious friends. He found partying each evening with the rowdies of the Honor Guard more appealing. Months passed. As he watched Terry's behavior and saw the changes occurring in Purdee's and Eric's lives, a conviction formed in his heart that he, too, needed this religion thing in his life.

When Kevin's mother, a Presbyterian, learned of her son's interest in what she considered a strange cult, she wrote letters trying to dissuade him from further involvement. Her letters didn't produce the results she desired, so she decided to visit him at the base.

Tight-lipped and armed with an arsenal of spiritual and emotional weapons, she arrived the week of Kevin's baptism at the Capitol Hill Church. Pastor Phipps was speaking at the

Sligo Church that Sabbath, but he arranged to come back to the Capitol Hill Church in order to perform the baptism. The church members overwhelmed the wary woman with love. After the service, Pastor and Mrs. Phipps invited Kevin, Kevin's mother, and his friends home for dinner. The hospitality of the church and the pastor's family really impressed her, changing her entire view. She returned home to witness to her parents.

"If it's God's will that I stay," Kevin reasoned, "then I'll stay. But if He provides me with a way to leave, I want to go." Three months later, the military agreed to discharge him.

Purdee had been watching his friends make decisions for Christ but just couldn't bring himself to make the same choice. "It involves too much sacrifice."

They had all heard of the offer he'd received from the State Department to help with the construction of a new embassy in South Africa at $50,000.00 a year. As a security policeman, his job would be to prevent the installation of eavesdropping devices, as occurred earlier in Moscow. "But they refuse to give me my Sabbaths off."

"We'll be praying for you, man." Eric gave Purdee's shoulder a gentle push. "What about you, Terry? You've already signed over twice for the Honor Guard. You gonna do it again?"

"They're pressuring me to. But I'm feeling more and more that, once I complete my original commitment to the air force, it will be time to move on." He thought for a moment, "You know, I'm actually getting excited about going to college now."

"Where? Walla Walla?" Eric asked.

"Probably. I've managed to save up enough money for the first year in an Adventist college, at least. Elder Phipps and others have suggested I attend Oakwood College in Alabama." Terry laughed again. "Did you know that I got a full scholarship from Oral Roberts University and one from Jimmy Swaggart Bible College too? When I told them I didn't believe their doctrines, they suggested I study psychology with them instead of religion. I don't know how they learned about me, but they did."

Chapter Thirty-five

The preparations for President-elect Bush's inauguration were well underway when Terry went to see the commander. Terry waited outside the commander's office, knowing he was about to ask the impossible. He was going to ask to be released from the air force three months early so he could assist in a major evangelistic series being conducted in a black neighborhood of Washington, D.C., by Elder W. C. Scales of the General Conference.

So much had happened since the Sabbath Terry, Purdee, and Eric attended the Sligo Church together. At the potluck, Terry met a pastor from Oregon assigned to Hadley Memorial Hospital who gave him his card and invited him to visit the hospital sometime. All the way back to the dormitory, Eric raved about the delicious vegetarian food he'd tasted at the potluck, so Terry decided he'd take Eric over to the hospital on the following Monday, since the hospital grounds sat back to back with Bolling Air Force Base.

The minister from Oregon welcomed them with a huge bear hug and introduced both men to the hospital chaplain, Elder Ebineezer Pedapudi. This introduction set off a chain of events that brought Terry to the attention of Elder W. C. Scales.

Elder Scales had been watching Terry week after week at the Capitol Hill Church. So when Elder Pedapudi suggested having Terry join them in the meetings, Elder Scales readily agreed. He would be in charge of the young people and help with evening Bible studies. When they asked Terry if he'd like to help out with the meetings, he eagerly agreed until he discovered how soon they'd need him. He reminded the two pastors of his military commitment. "Could you try to get an early release?" one of the men suggested. Terry agreed to at least ask, though he knew his chances were less than good.

Terry entered the commander's office and explained his request. "I am very familiar with the neighborhood where the meetings will be held since my friend, Eric Hayes, and I have been going down there all year, handing out lunches."

The commander studied Terry's face, then glanced down at the young man's records. "Give me time to review your records, Sergeant Johnson, and I'll let you know."

Later, when Terry received his early release, officially stamped and approved, he couldn't believe it. He hurried to tell his friends back at the dormitory. He would leave the Honor Guard and the air force soon after the inauguration exercises.

It was customary for the young honor guardsmen to handle most of the inauguration exercises, while the old-timers, Terry's classification once he made sergeant, were assigned to the more coveted function, President Reagan's farewell to the military held at Andrews Air Force Base. Considered a pro-military President, Reagan would be honored by all five branches of the service. His last official act as commander in chief of the United States would be to review and bid farewell to those who served with him during his eight years in office.

As NCO in charge, Terry hurried about the gigantic hangar, checking his men to be certain the cordons were in place and his men were ready to usher in the spouses of the government and military dignitaries. Organizing and maneuvering more than 600 people to the correct reserved areas took all of his attention. Also inside the hangar, United States *Air Force One* and the President's helicopter sat proudly on display, along with one sample of each plane and helicopter approved by Reagan during his presidency. The coast guard also displayed samples of their new drug-fighting boats.

For security purposes, all the guests were seated an hour

before the President's 2:00 p.m. arrival. The cordoned seating areas included a special section for representatives and senators, foreign ambassadors, and cabinet members. Top brass from the Pentagon sat in a special area to one side of the dais, with the press corps sitting on the far side of the dais. The grandstand was filled with air force personnel, their spouses, and their children, as well as other high-ranking military officials. Terry always kept one eye on the press corps. He never knew when an overeager photographer might step into the "no man's land" between the crowd and the President while he stood at the lectern.

News that the President's helicopter had landed reached Terry only seconds before the entire gathering learned of it. On cue, four lines of honor guardsmen formed their cordon of rifles. Terry stood at the end of the front line, closest to the dais, still keeping an eye out to be certain the press didn't violate their parameters. When the air force band struck the first notes of "Hail to the Chief," he felt cold chills run the length of his spine. The thrill had intensified instead of lessened over the more than three years he'd served with the guard.

President Reagan and his Secret Service men walked the length of the corridor of honor guardsmen. Distracted for a moment by a photographer who'd come into his peripheral vision, when Terry's thoughts returned to the task at hand, the President was within three feet of him. On impulse, Terry snapped off a smart salute. President Reagan stopped and saluted back. The President's unplanned gesture triggered the audience to break into an unbridled ovation, screaming and applauding as the President continued his walk to the lectern.

When President Reagan raised his hands for silence, the audience obliged. Tears misted in the retiring President's eyes as he spoke fondly of his years as commander in chief. Secretary of Defense Carlucci awarded him a service medal and pinned it on the President's suit pocket. The Honor Guard performed a special "present arms" as Reagan reviewed them for the last time as President. Before leaving the hangar, President Reagan turned and called out, "I'm proud of you all," then gave a thumbs-up sign and boarded the helicopter for his short trip back to the White House.

That night, as Terry unwound from the excitement of the day, he realized that in a little less than four years, he'd met more heads of state than any member of Congress or even Vice President Bush, for that matter. He realized he'd been given opportunities about which most military men only dream. Who would have imagined the chain of events that followed his innocent inquiry at the air force recruiter's booth at the mall next to Portland Adventist Academy? Who would have imagined the walls God had helped him clear, the doors God had opened—doors Terry hadn't known existed?

He felt strangely out of place on President-elect George Bush's inauguration day, January 20. He was used to giving the orders, directing the young guardsmen. On this day, all he could do was stand and watch as a younger NCO shouted the commands.

The pale winter-solstice sun shone down on the Capitol steps as, out of habit, Terry's disciplined eyes surveyed the area reserved for the members of the President's Cabinet and for foreign dignitaries. He noticed the back of one folding chair facing the platform was slightly crooked. It took determined concentration to avoid ordering an airman nearby to straighten it.

The entire inauguration week had been carefully choreographed. For three weeks the members of the President's Honor Guard had prepared for the inauguration of America's forty-first President. Army, marine corps, navy, air force, and coast guard—all five divisions of the Honor Guard—would be highly visible. Some would march in the parade from the White House to the west front of the Capitol. Some would fire the twenty-one gun salute. Others would carry flags. Sergeant Johnson's unit would escort government officials and their spouses to their appropriate seats as well as maintain crowd control.

The biting January wind whipped through the cordoned area with a fury. Terry fought the urge to burrow deep into his lightweight wool Honor Guard blouse. Terry's medals glistened in the sunlight as he watched and listened to the new members of the corps review the day's responsibilities.

The corps had been busy since 4:00 a.m. making last-minute arrangements for the ceremony. For old times' sake, Terry bounded up the steps to the area where the new President would be sworn in. He glanced down over the twenty-foot wall that would separate the new President from the crowd of dignitaries and members of the press seated below. A thrill coursed through him as he strode across to the speaker's lectern.

In a very short time, George Bush, the newly elected President of the United States, would take his oath of office—a thirty-four word affirmation: "I do solemnly swear that I will execute the office of President of the United States and will, to the best of my ability, preserve, protect, and defend the Constitution of the United States." Bush's inaugural address would follow.

Terry scanned the area one last time as people began arriving for the ceremony. He noted the first guardsmen already escorting the wife of some government dignitary to her reserved seat. Off to one side, a Secret Service man with a walkie-talkie reported that the procession would arrive shortly.

The sounds of excited children laughing and chattering with one another suddenly filled the area. Terry spun about to see what seemed like hordes of children ascending the Capitol steps. Where are all these kids coming from? he thought. They shouldn't be here—not now, not minutes before the President's entourage arrives.

"It's all right, sergeant." One of the security park police standing in the group chuckled. "They're Bush's grandkids."

Terry watched the Bush family assemble on the stage. The man who was about to become President of the United States bent close to one of the younger girls, listening intently to the child's every word.

Dressed in a bright blue wool coat, Mrs. Bush helped her daughters and daughters-in-law corral the children into their places, taking the time to pat down one young Bush's cowlick before the ceremony began. Relatives and neighbors of the family gathered on the stage along with the nation's top senators and prominent religious leaders. Terry recognized the faces of Robert Schuller, Billy Graham, and Norman Vincent Peale.

Terry and his friend, Sergeant Griffey, stood off to one side, ready to move in should a situation arise that would call for extra backup. Griffey had left and rejoined the Honor Guard a number of times during his career in the air force. This was the third inauguration he had attended as a guardsman.

"Just like the Carter inauguration," Griffey whispered to Terry. "Carter's inauguration was a family affair too. Now, President Reagan's, that was another matter." Griffey described Reagan's inauguration as a high-class society event. "His rich friends were carefully positioned for photo sessions."

The reserved seating area filled quickly and smoothly. The press corps scrambled into their cordoned-off area. Television cameras blinked on, and microphones came to life. The cast lined up across the stage behind George Bush and the chief justice of the United States.

As the chief justice of the Supreme Court of the United States administered the oath of office, news reporters captured the changing expressions on the faces of those on stage. Terry recorded them in his memory—Barbara Bush's look of dignity and calm, the children and grandchildren's gazes of wonder and admiration. The look of pride on the face of George Bush's mother, a look very similar to the one his own mother wore whenever one of her children brought honor to the family.

He choked back the tears of pride at the thought of his mother in Oregon—the determined woman who refused to allow the educational system to throw her son away. One by one, Terry remembered family, teachers, ministers, and friends who'd given him so much. His list of gratitude seemed endless.

Terry noticed tears glistening in Ronald Reagan's eyes as the new president turned and saluted the former President for a job well done. For a moment, Terry felt at one with the man. Terry's heart ached, knowing that his time with the Honor

Guard was coming to an end. While he had lived nearly four years instead of eight at the center of this world's power, Terry could only imagine how Mr. Reagan must have felt, about to step back into the plain, everyday world of the average citizen. What would the future hold for this man who'd given his country so many years of service, and what was the future to be for the country he'd served? What did Terry's own future hold, for that matter? College? Which college? Pastor? Youth leader? Evangelist? The uncertainties caused a tremor of fear to enter his mind.

He returned his attention to the new President and the inaugural address.

"The new breeze blows, a page turns, the story unfolds—and so today a chapter begins . . ." (Inauguration speech, George Bush—Washington, D.C., 1989).

A chapter closes, and a new one begins. Terry liked that. He felt his worries and concerns over the future lift from his shoulders. There's really nothing to fear, he reminded himself, as long as I remember who is writing the book.

Epilogue

When God promises to exalt His name through mere humans, He does it with style. God singled out Terry to become the first handicapped (dyslexic) person ever recorded to serve in the President's Honor Guard, as well as the first black guardsman from his home state of Oregon. He is the first practicing Seventh-day Adventist to be chosen for the guard. His tour of duty was extended twice, as was his appointment to the Pentagon. He was awarded twelve badges, medals, and citations in less than four years. He served as treasurer of the Honor Guard Association as well as on the Bolling Air Force Base Unit Advisory Council for two years.

In 1988, Terry received the Outstanding Young Men of America Award, a national nonmilitary award for community service. In the process, Terry's dream of having one person from each Honor Guard unit baptized was realized. Terry did his part also. He presented 157 individual series of Bible studies, twelve lessons each. Twenty-four have been baptized as of this writing. All of this was accomplished by a black, dyslexic young man who had once been declared too retarded to educate in the state school system and by a God who knew better.

While Terry's story is about one young man's victory over incredible odds, it is also a victory for committed teachers. Who could ever imagine the damage a teacher inflicts on a child by labeling him as dumb, retarded, stupid, a troublemaker? Who can believe the miracles a teacher can produce by building up one child's faith in himself and in God? And who can comprehend the silent influence Christian teachers can have on the pupils they face every day?

The next chapter of Terry's adventure has been as exciting as the rest. During the meetings held in the Disctrict of Columbia the summer following his departure from the military, 138 people were baptized. After his freshman year at Oakwood College, Terry assisted in a second series of meetings, this time held in Alabama, where 110 were baptized. On May 27, 1991, Terry left with Elder Scales's evangelistic team for West Africa for a six-week series of meetings in Ghana. He plans to return to Oakwood College for his junior year as a theology/communications major in the fall. Woven into this busy lifestyle, Terry works at the college radio station as a newscaster and on weekends travels all over the country, speaking to churches and youth groups.

Where are the other principal characters in Terry's story? As of this writing,

1. Staff Sergeant Collier's entire life has changed. He has become the new cadets' favorite basic training instructor. The strongest words he uses on his trainees is "You meatball!"

2. Jeff, Terry's friend from basic training and from the police academy, is baptized, married, and stationed in Korea.

3. Tom, Terry's other buddy from basic training, has continued his Bible studies with Adventists near his station in Grand Forks, North Dakota, where he attends the local SDA church.

4. Frank, Terry's Mormon roommate in T-flight, was baptized and lives with his wife and children in Garden Grove, California.

5. Carl was baptized and left the military due to Sabbath-observance problems.

6. Sergeant Dan Eddings left the military and is working on his theology degree at a Nazarene college.

7. Sergeant Reggie Washington married and is stationed in Florida.

8. Sergeant "Coop" Cooper left the military and works for a corporation in the Washington, D.C., area and has continued his studies with the "Breath of Life" program.

9. Wes, the guardsman who flaked on the White House steps, is a state trooper in New York State. Both he and his wife are professed Christians.

10. Al and Sandy have continued their Bible studies at their new station in Maine.

11. John Banks was transferred to an outpost in Korea. Cathy took the children back to her home in Montana.

12. Mrs. Taylor, the bank teller, went on to become a bank manager.

13. Sergeant Casillo organized his NCO prep school in Hawaii and continues his Bible studies there.

14. Sergeant Griffey attends the Capitol Hill Church in Washington, D.C.

And from the letters Terry receives regularly from all over the world, he knows that God hasn't closed the book on his White House ministry. Terry believes that the final tally will be totaled on the other side.